The dance around the golden calf by Lucas van Leyden

Jan Piet Filedt Kok

Rijksmuseum / Nieuw Amsterdam

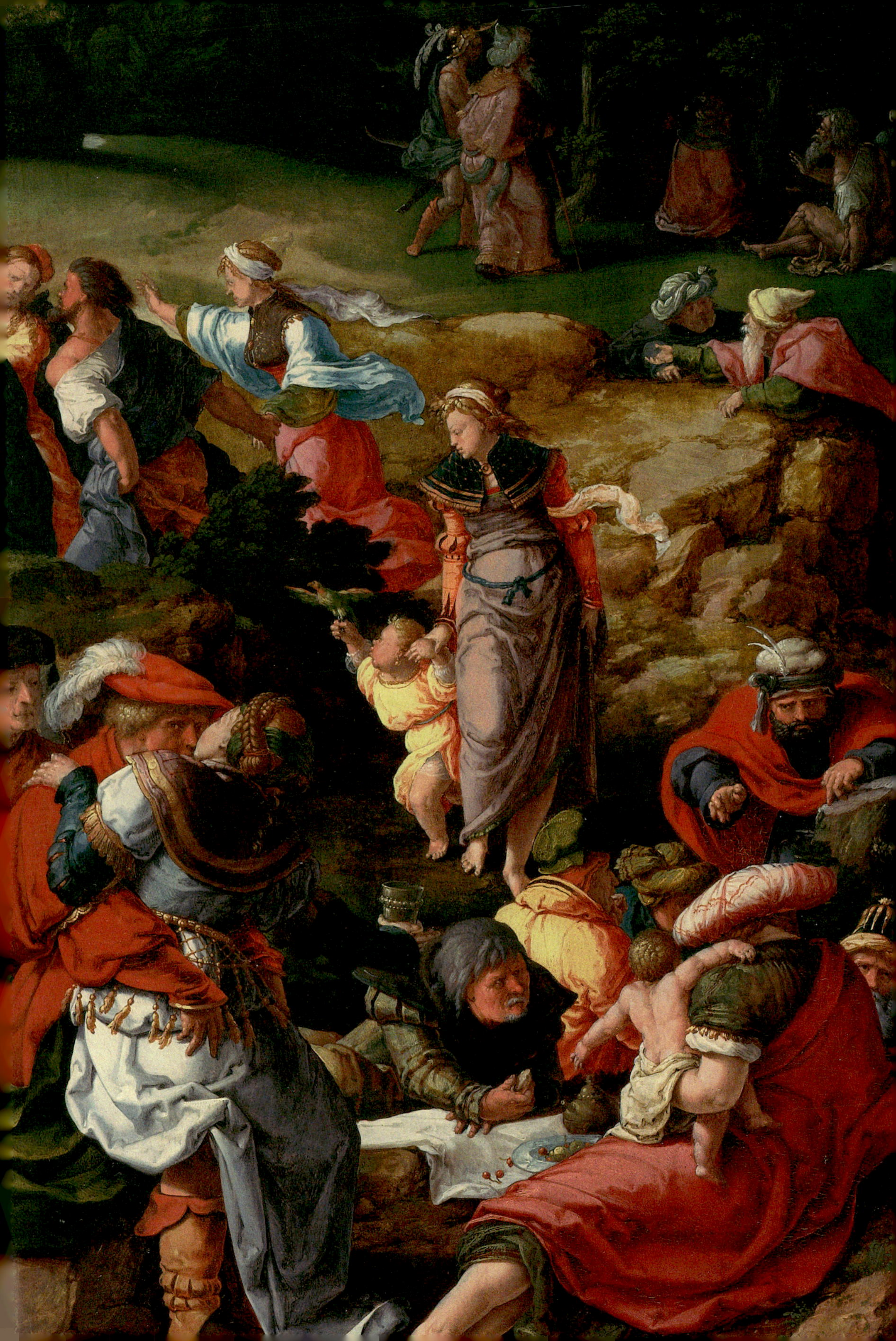

Contents

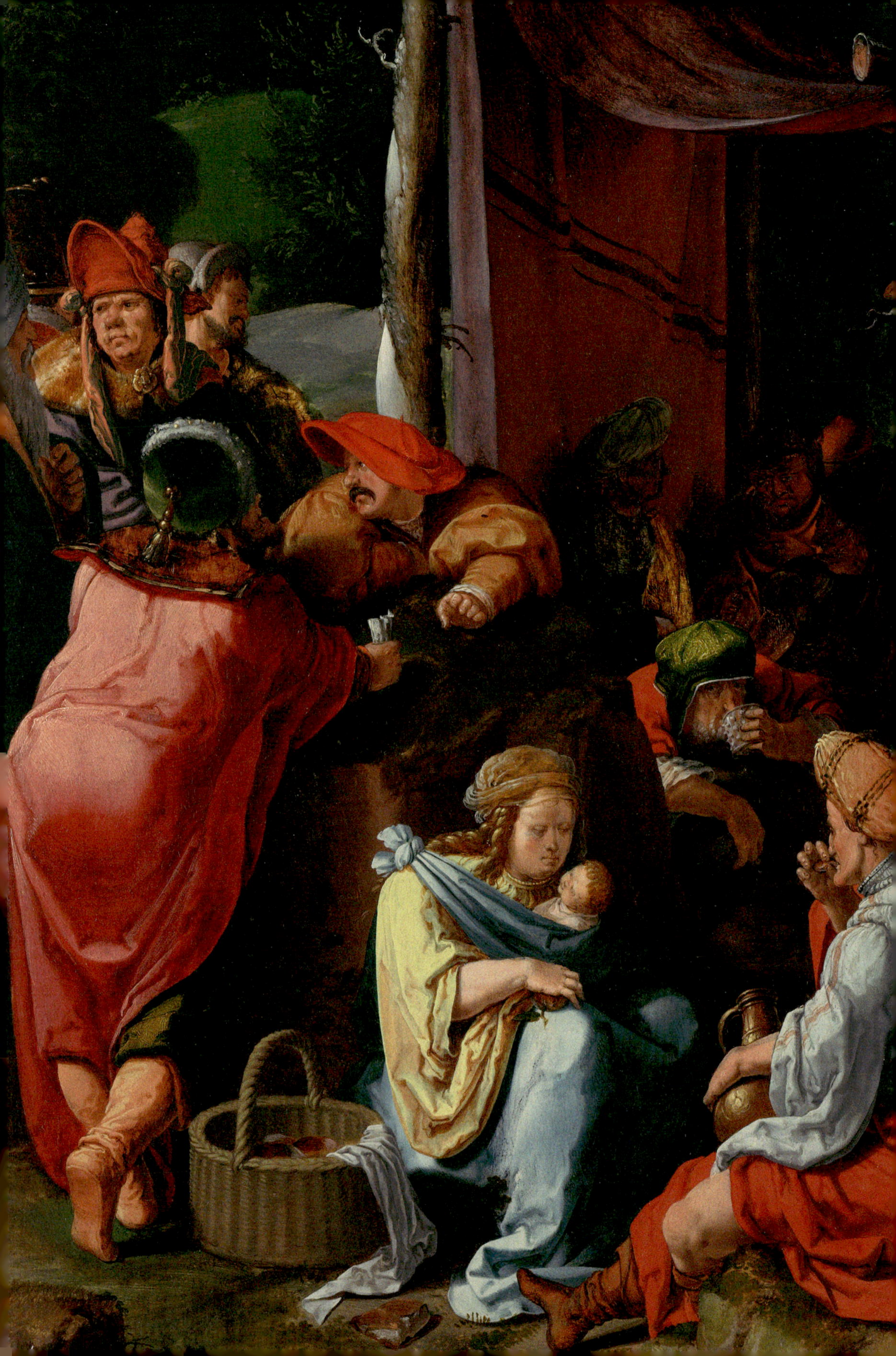

The rediscovery of a masterpiece

Some paintings so self-evidently belong in a particular museum that one can barely imagine it without them. That is also true of the triptych, *The dance around the golden calf*, which the Rijksmuseum acquired in 1952 by a happy coincidence. Dr Arthur van Schendel (1910-77, the chief curator of the Department of Paintings, who went on to become Director-General of the Rijksmuseum, had studied art history in Paris in the 1930s. After the war he returned there quite regularly to visit museums, art dealers and exhibitions and to meet colleagues. On one of those trips he was told about the estate of a widow, Madame Bignier, which might contain paintings that would be of interest to the Rijksmuseum. Although house calls of that kind are often fruitless, Van Schendel went to Madame Bignier's Paris apartment. The electricity had already been cut off, so he used a pocket torch to inspect the pictures. One that caught his eye was a triptych in an ebony frame (fig. 54), which at first he thought had been painted by Aertgen van Leyden (1498-1564). I.Q. van Regteren Altena (1899-1980), Van Schendel's colleague in the Amsterdam printroom, had published several lengthy articles on this Leiden contemporary of Lucas van Leyden in 1939, and in 1946 the Rijksmuseum had bought a painting of his, *The raising of Lazarus*.

Van Schendel was allowed to take the triptych back to Amsterdam for further investigation, where it was soon discovered that Karel van Mander had described it in his *Schilder-boeck* of 1604 in 'The life of Lucas van Leyden'. That description leaves no doubt as to the identification of the painting discovered in Paris. 'There is also a very excellent, more important piece or cabinet by Lucas in Amsterdam in Kalverstraat, being the story of the children of Israel dancing around the golden calf, in which they are sitting feasting in accordance with the text of the Scriptures, where it is said: The people sat down to eat and to drink, and rose up to play. At this banquet one sees the sensual appearance of the people and the impure desires revealed in their eyes depicted in a very lively manner.'

The triptych is documented several times in the seventeenth century in various Amsterdam collections, with a final mention in an auction catalogue of 1709. It surfaced again in 1870 at the Paris sale of the estate of the Marquis de Blaisel as a first-rate painting by Lucas van Leyden. From then on the scholarly literature on the artist made not a single mention of the original.

Once it had become clear that the work discovered by Van Schendel was the triptych described by Van Mander, the Rijksmuseum decided to enter into negotiations immediately. In June 1952 it bought the painting from Madame Bignier's heirs for the fairly modest sum of 2.8 million francs, a little over 30,000 guilders (less than 14,000 euros). After the yellowed varnish had

1
Detail of the left wing.

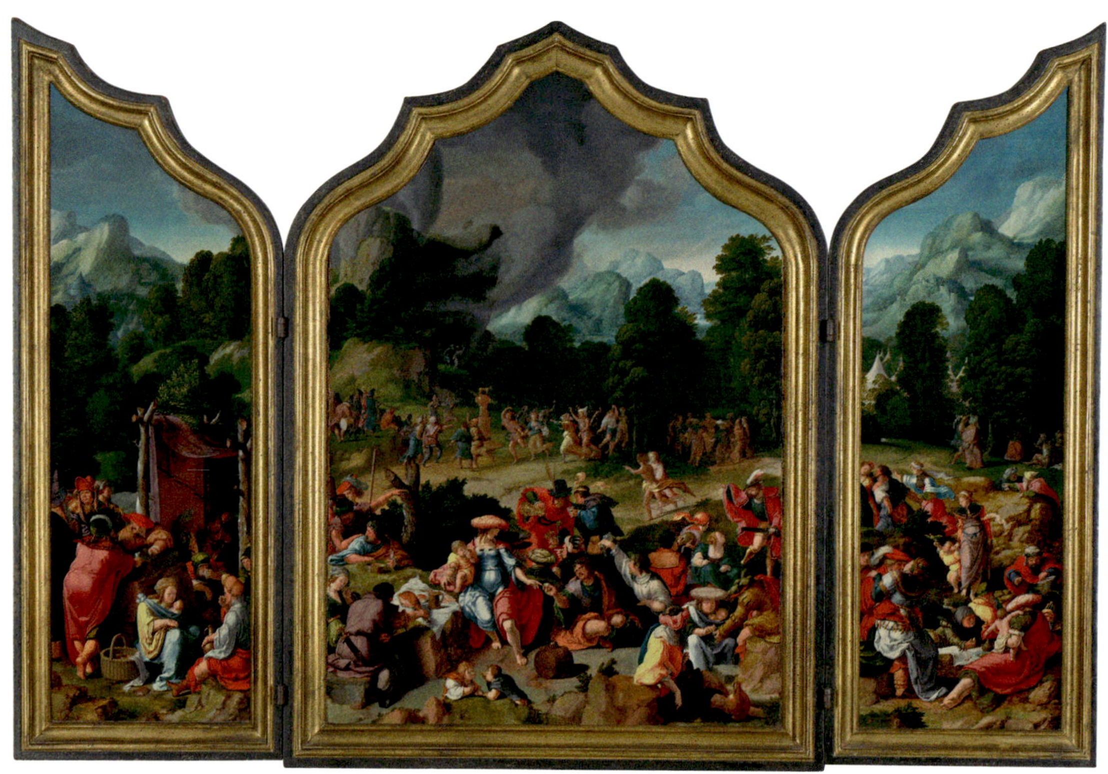

2
Lucas van Leyden, *Triptych with the dance around the golden calf*, c. 1530. Oil on panel, centre panel: 93 x 67 cm, wings: 91 x 30 cm. Rijksmuseum, Amsterdam. The triptych in the frame made for it in 1952 by the frame maker Heijdenrijk. Gilt and painted black, it was an imitation of a sixteenth-century frame, and its surface was treated to make it look old.

been removed in the museum's conservation studio it could be seen that the painting was in excellent condition. A number of Lucas van Leyden specialists shared in the enthusiasm about the rediscovery. One of them, Nicolaas Beets (1878-1963), published an article about it in the *Algemeen Handelsblad* of 23 September 1952, and contributed a lengthier essay to the art history journal *Oud Holland* that same year. Arthur van Schendel wrote an article in the first issue of the *Bulletin van het Rijksmuseum* of 1953 under the title 'Lucas van Leyden's "Dans om het gouden kalf" terug in Amsterdam' (Lucas van Leyden's *Dance around the golden calf* back in Amsterdam), thus confirming the rediscovery of Lucas van Leyden's masterpiece. The triptych, in a newly made frame, was given a prominent position in the Rijksmuseum's permanent display in the autumn of 1952 (fig. 2).

The Old Testament story

The triptych depicts one of the key moments in the Old Testament. The book of Exodus relates how the people of Israel disobeyed God's commandment by erecting a statue of a golden calf in the Sinai desert, and gave themselves over to feasting in the absence of their leader Moses (Exodus 32). Lucas van Leyden showed himself to be a gifted storyteller in his triptych, depicting the event in an entertaining way. In order to understand the scene it is worth summarising the biblical narrative and what preceded it, and trying to discover what the painting meant for the artist's contemporaries.

THE BIBLICAL TEXT

The book of Genesis ends with the story of Joseph, who had settled in Egypt with his family, the Israelites. The next book of the Bible, Exodus, tells how his descendants, a growing number of Israelites, were persecuted after his death. They decided to leave Egypt after having been there 400 years, under the leadership of Moses and his brother Aaron, despite the opposition of the Pharaoh, the king of Egypt. Pursued by his armies they managed to escape, because God parted the Red Sea so that they could pass through, and then let the waters fall back on themselves to drown the pursuers. 'Thus the LORD saved Israel that day out of the hand of the Egyptians, [...] and the people feared the LORD, and believed the LORD, and his servant Moses', are the closing words of Exodus 14. The Israelites' journey through the desert was full of hardship, hunger and thirst. God finally came to their aid with the rain of manna, food that fell from the skies (Exodus 16), and with water struck from a rock (Exodus 17) (see fig. 27). After the Israelites had defeated the tribe of Amalek, they arrived at the Sinai desert in the third month after leaving Egypt, where they pitched camp. God then commanded Moses to climb Mount Sinai on his own, and appeared to him in the form of a thick cloud. He gave Moses detailed instructions for the people of Israel and laid down a series of laws and moral and religious commandments. This is the moment when the Jewish religion was given shape and rules. God finally gave Moses two stone tablets with the Ten Commandments written with God's finger (Exodus 31:18), moral precepts that also apply to Christians.

Moses stayed on Mount Sinai for 40 days and 40 nights. The Israelites were worried by his long absence, and demanded that his brother Aaron give them back the gods of Egypt. In order to nip the rebellion in the bud, Aaron ordered them to bring him all their gold earrings, which he melted down and had cast in a statue in the form of a calf. The Bible relates that when the people called out, 'These be thy gods, O Israel, which brought thee up out of the land of Egypt', Aaron built an altar before it and announced that the following day would be 'a feast to the

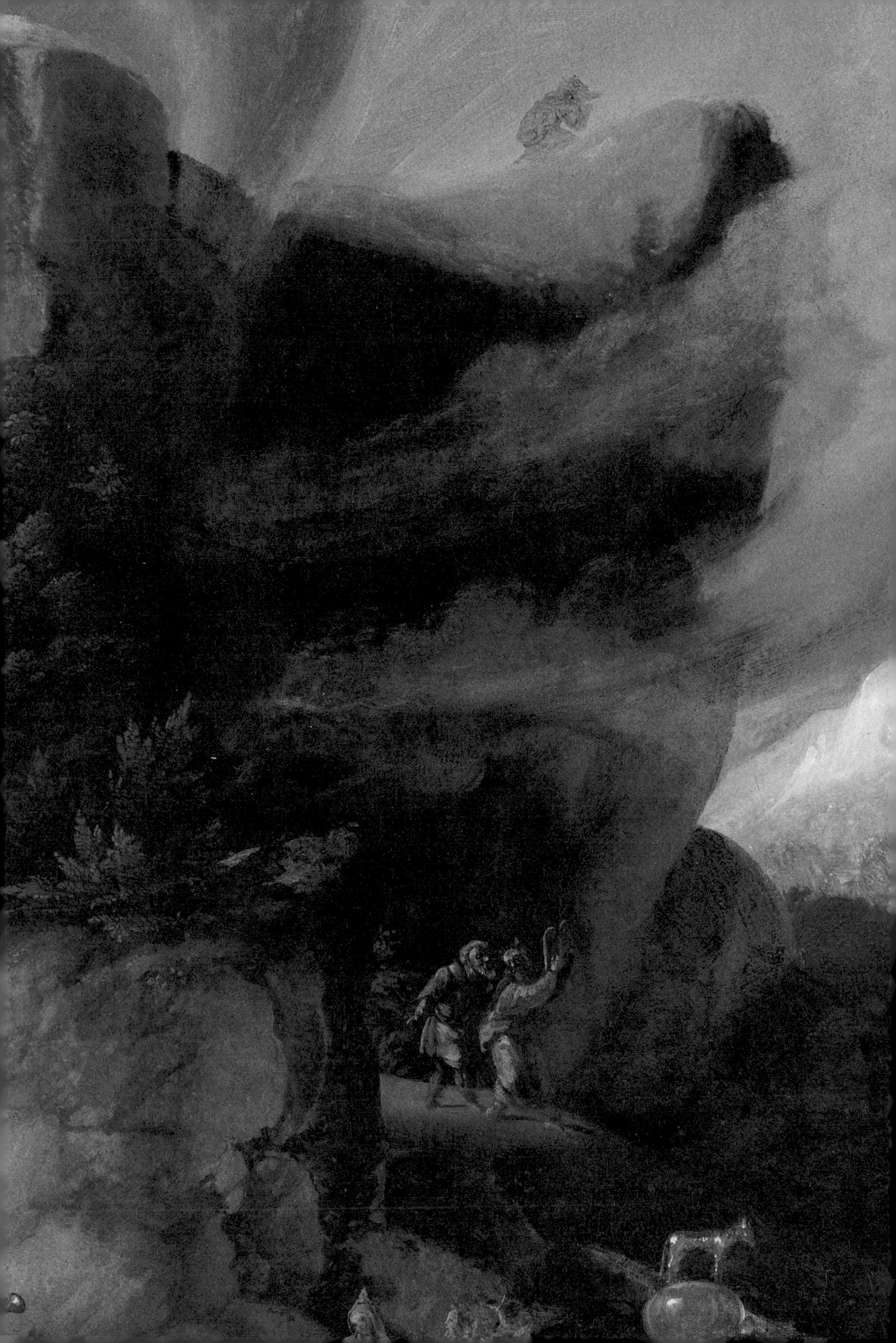

3
Detail of the top left quarter of the centre panel. The minuscule figure kneeling on the projecting rock is Moses, to whom God appeared 'in a thick cloud'. He is seen a second time further down the mountain with his servant Joshua at the moment when he sees the idolatry of his people and throws away the stone tablets of the law in a rage. Below him the people are dancing around the golden calf.

LORD'. The Bible continues: 'And they rose up early on the morrow, and offered burnt offerings, and brought peace offerings; and the people sat down to eat and to drink, and rose up to play'. God saw this, and said to Moses: 'Go, get thee down; for thy people, which thou broughtest out of the land of Egypt, have corrupted themselves: They have turned aside quickly out of the way which I commanded them'. Moses came down from the mountain with the stone tablets of the law. As he approached the camp, he saw the golden statue and the dancing, and in a fury hurled the tablets to the ground at the foot of the mountain, smashing them into pieces. He threw the golden statue into the fire and ground it into powder. He then gathered together all the Israelites who were on the Lord's side and ordered them to kill all the others, 'and slay every man his brother, and every man his companion, and every man his neighbour'. Some 3,000 Israelites perished that day (Exodus 32:1-20). Moses then prayed for his people, and God forgave them. He went back up the mountain, where God reappeared to him and again wrote on two stone tablets (Exodus 33-34).

THE DANCE DEPICTED BY LUCAS

There is far more to the story than that, but the passages cited above are the ones that Lucas depicted in his triptych. Moses can be seen in the centre panel as a minuscule figure kneeling on a projecting finger of rock high up on the mountain, surrounded by dense clouds, for as the Bible puts it, God appeared to him 'in a thick cloud'.
He appears again a little further down, this time with his servant Joshua, at the very moment when he sees the idolatry of his people and throws the tablets to the ground in a rage (fig. 3). Below that, still in the background on the centre panel, is a group of musicians on the left, boisterous couples dancing around the calf in the centre, and beneath the trees on the right a group of people performing a round dance (fig. 4).
The main subject of the festive Israelites is set in the foreground landscape, which runs across all three panels. The licentious behaviour of the people of Israel, who are disobeying God's commandment by surrendering themselves to unbridled merrymaking, dancing, lovemaking, eating and drinking, is depicted in a remarkably varied way, with a colourful crowd of mothers with children, young people and the elderly seated on the ground, but above all in motion (fig. 6). The prominent figure group in the middle, where a woman in a large hat with a child on her lap is offering a piece of fruit to a man (fig. 6) recalls the Fall of Man. This suggests that ignoring God's commandment is equivalent to indulging in sensual pleasures.
The colourful clothing, headgear and turbans give the crowd an oriental look, and Lucas's contemporaries would have associated the many feathers and plumes with frivolous and vain behaviour.

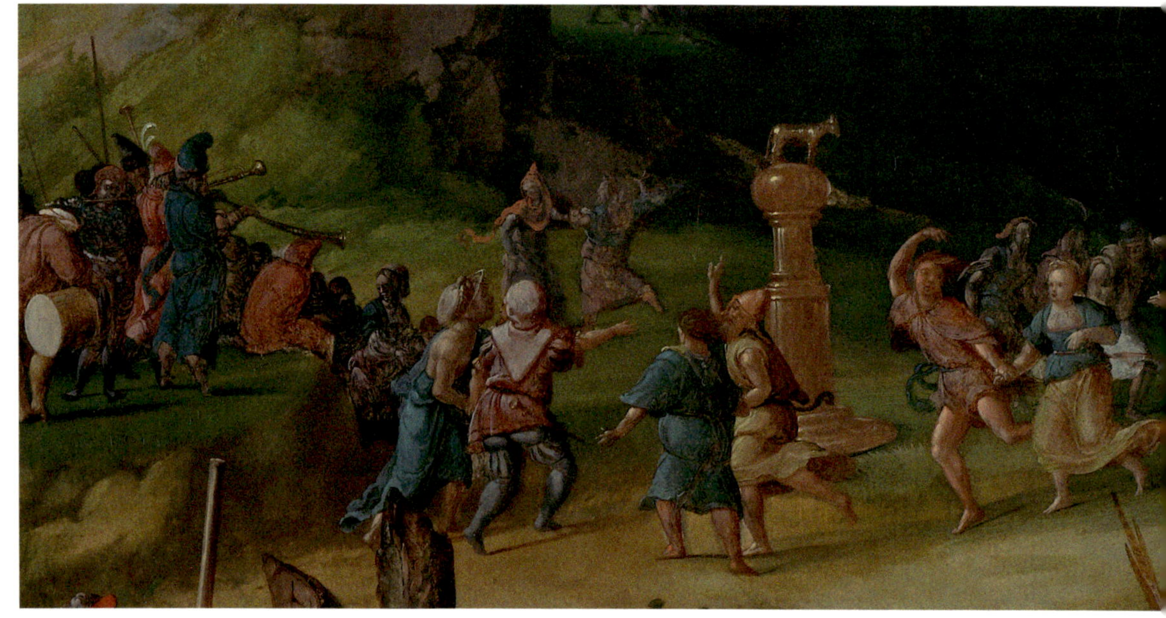

4
The middleground of the centre panel: a group of musicians with drum and shawms, and figures dancing around the golden calf.

THE ICONOGRAPHIC TRADITION

Depicting Old Testament subjects was a new departure in early sixteenth-century Dutch painting, and Lucas van Leyden was one of the first to do so. Moses, the leader and lawmaker of the Jewish people, is traditionally seen as a precursor of Christ. *The dance around the golden calf* had already been depicted in that context in Italian art. Two fresco cycles by Botticelli, Ghirlandaio, Rosselli and Perugino of c. 1480-1490 in the Sistine Chapel show the life of Moses and the life of Christ on two facing walls, while Cosimo Rosselli's *Dance around the golden calf* of c. 1488 is directly opposite *The sermon on the mount* (Matthew 5-7). This was deliberate, for Christ quoted the Ten Commandments in his sermon. The depiction of Old Testament scenes in Netherlandish art was stimulated when, in Antwerp in 1582, Willem Vorsterman published a complete translation of the Bible into Dutch, based on Luther's translation. However, the tradition of depicting Old Testament scenes as harbingers of events in the New Testament originated far earlier in book illumination. In the fifteenth century and at the beginning of the sixteenth this gave rise to block books illustrated with woodcuts, such as the *Speculum Humanis Salvationis* and the *Biblia Pauperum*, in which Moses's destruction of the golden calf was presented as a prefiguration of the fall of the Egyptian idols when Mary, Joseph and the infant Christ fled to Egypt. Both the Old Testament and New Testament scenes make it clear that it was no longer permitted to worship idols.

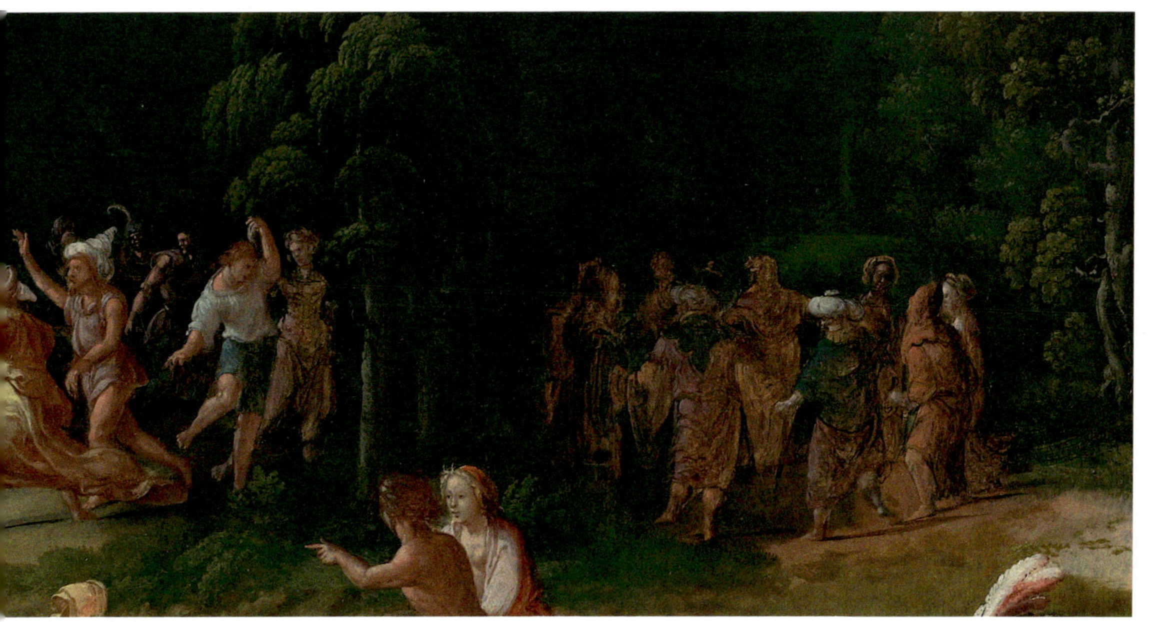

5
Lucas Cranach, *The dance around the golden calf* with Moses receiving the tables of the law, c. 1527. Woodcut, 11.5 x 7.5 cm, in Luther's *Deutsche Catechismus* of 1529.

Starting in the late middle ages, it was also customary for Old Testament stories to be used as moral illustrations of the Ten Commandments, with the dance around the golden calf serving as the traditional example of breaking the first commandment, 'Thou shalt have no other gods before me'. The combination of Moses receiving the tables of the law and the dance around the golden calf was depicted several times in fifteenth and sixteenth-century cycles of Old Testament exempla of the Ten Commandments. That tradition was strengthened even further by the iconography of the Reformation. One example of this is the woodcuts by Lucas Cranach that illustrate transgressions of the Ten Commandments in Luther's *Deutsche Catechismus* of 1529. There, too, the dance around the golden calf and Moses receiving the

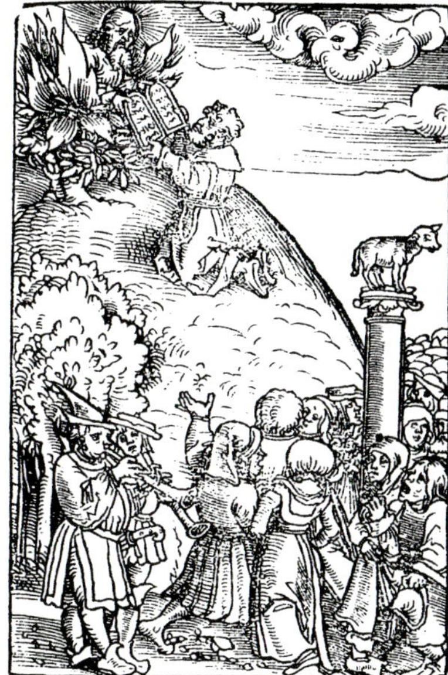

6 >>
Lower half of the centre panel, with people eating and feasting.

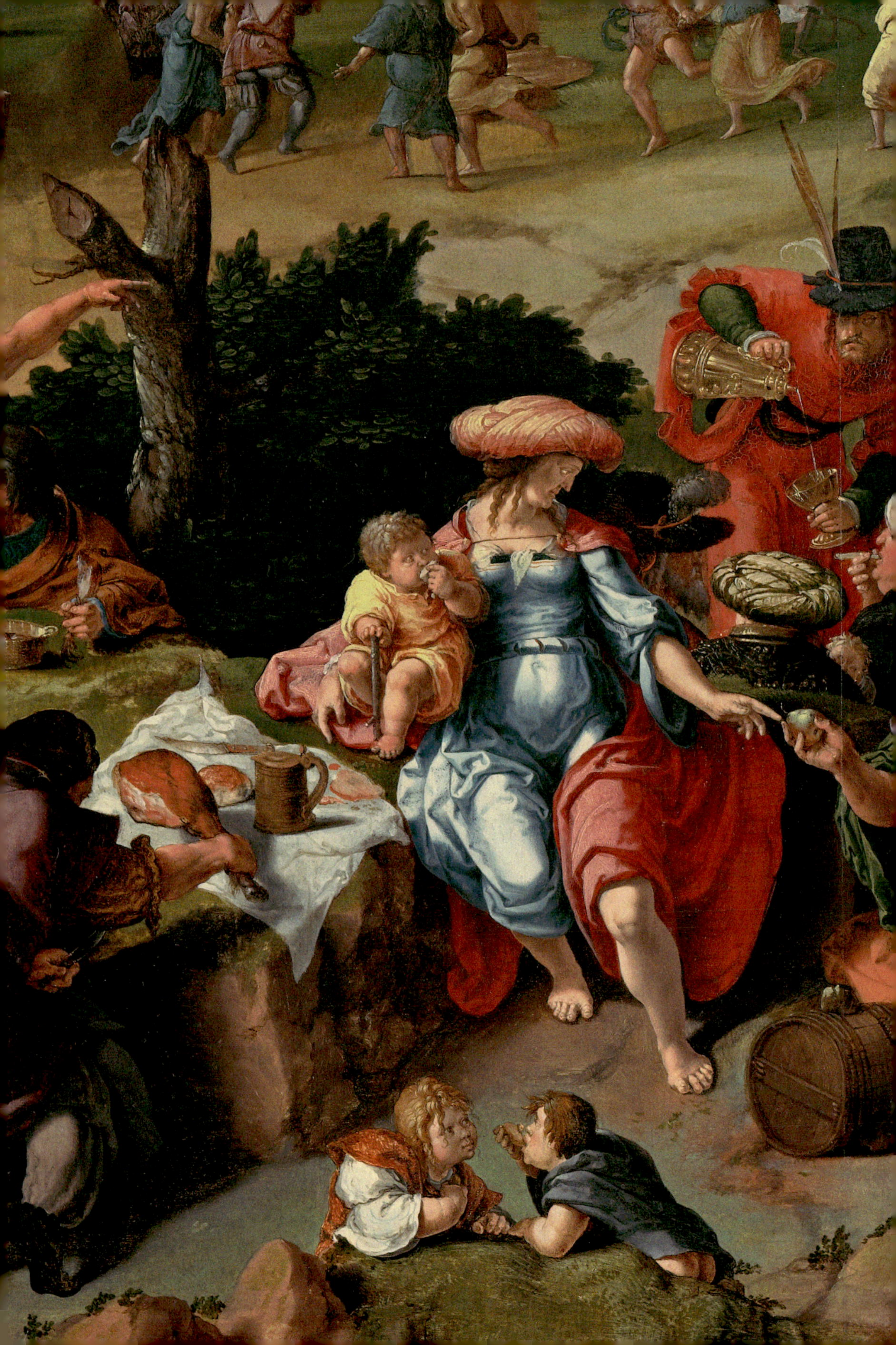

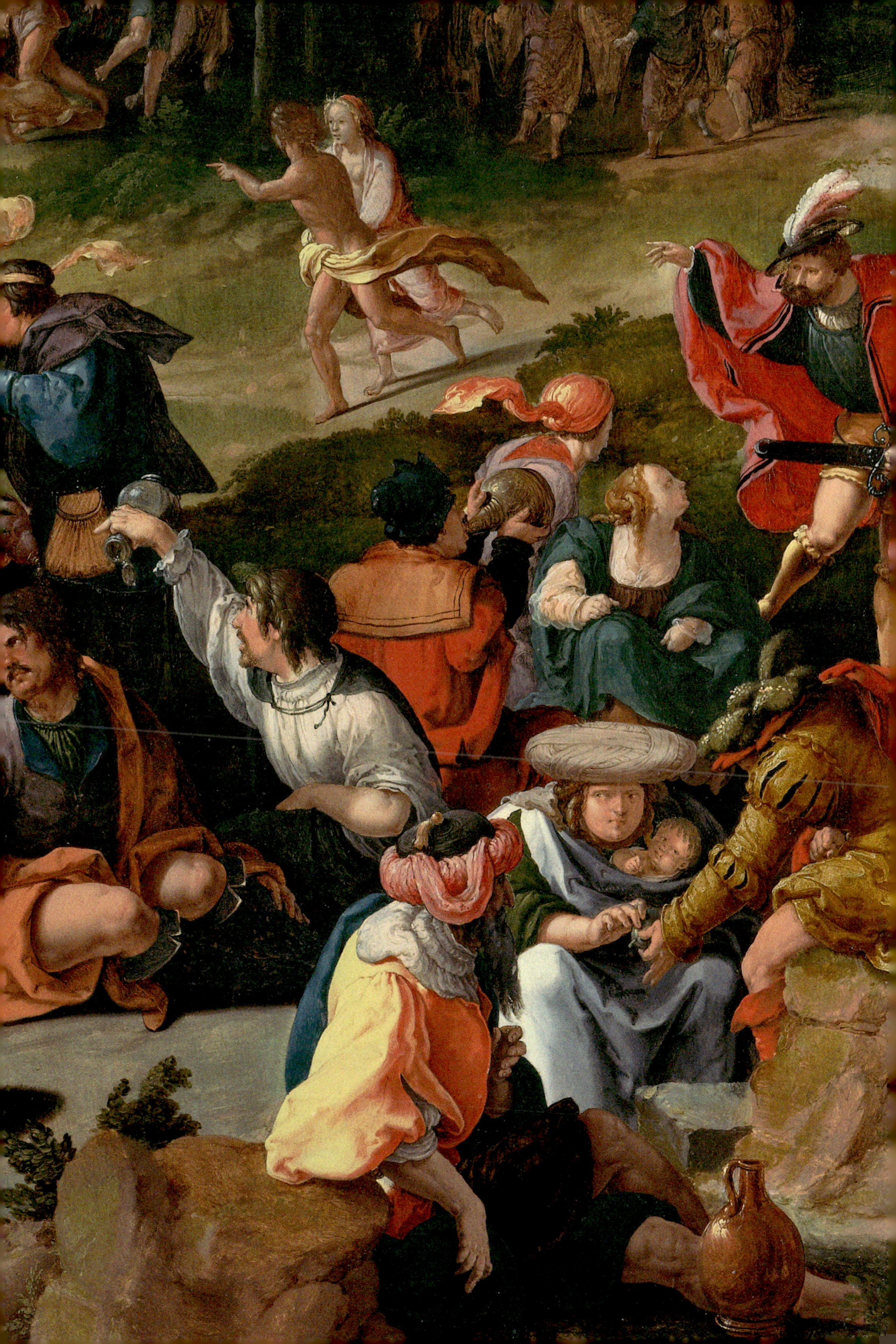

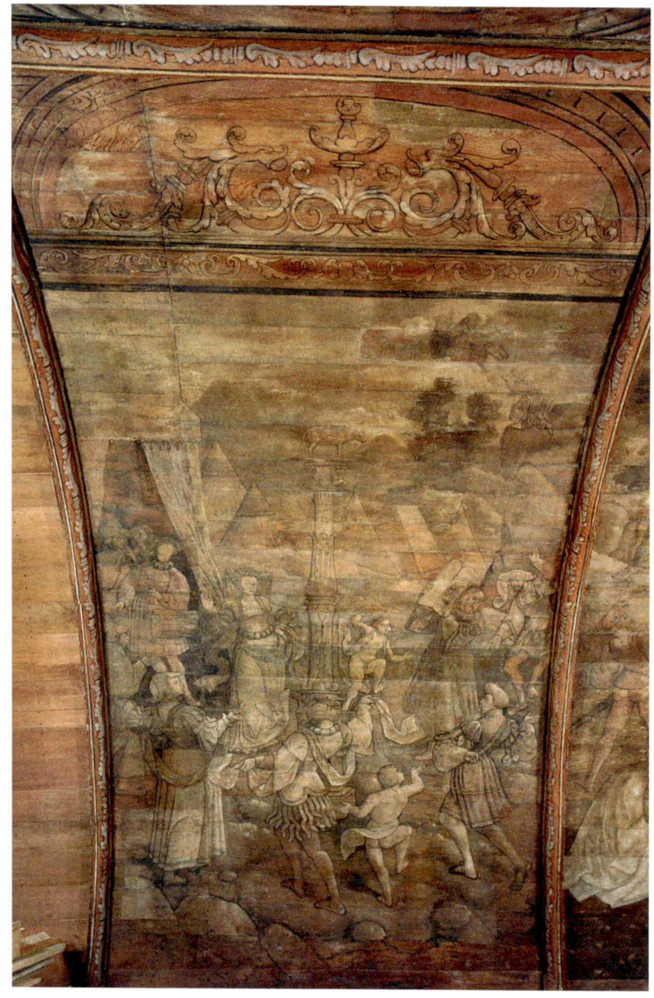

7
Workshop of Jacob Cornelisz van Oostsanen, *The dance around the golden calf*, c. 1530. Hervormde Kerk, Warmenhuizen. A few Dutch churches still have monumental ceiling paintings dating from the early sixteenth century. On the choir vault in a small church in the province of North Holland, north of Alkmaar, there are scenes of four Old Testament subjects – the passage through the Red Sea, the rain of manna, the meeting of Abraham and Melchizedek, and the dance around the golden calf – combined with the *Last Judgement*. A similar *Last Judgement* in the Grote Kerk in Alkmaar was also designed by the Amsterdam painter Jacob Cornelisz van Oostsanen.

tables of the law (fig. 5) are an example of breaking the first commandment. A *Dance around the golden calf* in the church at Warmenhuizen in the province of North Holland can be dated around 1530, in the period when Lucas painted his triptych. The ceiling paintings for this church were very probably designed by Jacob Cornelisz van Oostsanen, and show the Last Judgement and four Old Testament scenes, including the dance. In it (fig. 7) we see Moses receiving the tables from God and breaking them when he catches sight of the people dancing. The emphasis is on the jubilation around the pillar with the calf, where the dancers, children and sumptuously attired figures stress the folly and lasciviousness of the festivities. The combination of the Last Judgement and the dance around the golden calf in this vault painting is not a coincidence, for we know that breaking the first commandment is punished with death.

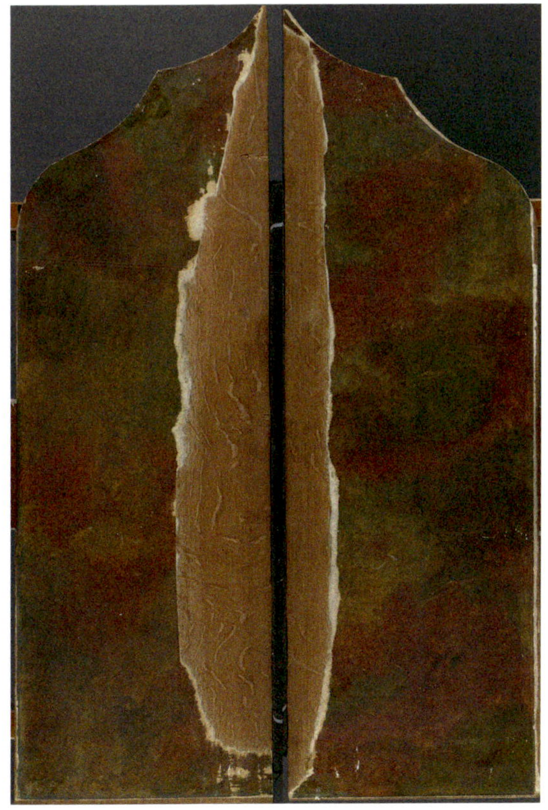

8
The outer wings of the *Triptych with the dance around the golden calf*, which are decorated with red-green marbling on a white ground. After the wings had been removed from their original frames they were sawn down a little at the top and some of the paint was shaved off to fit them in the ebony frame, which completely concealed the backs of the panels.

WARNING AGAINST THE WORSHIP OF STRANGE GODS AND DEBAUCHERY

Lucas van Leyden's triptych was undoubtedly a warning against breaking the first commandment by worshipping idols, and against immoral behaviour in general, and was thus an exhortation to live according to God's commandments. That moral was an excuse for the evident pleasure with which Lucas painted this biblical story, drawing the viewer into the scene. The triptych probably did not serve a public function, for the outsides of the wings are not adorned with a painting but are decorated with red and green imitation marbling (fig. 8). The intention must have been to have the triptych hung up opened, probably in the home of a wealthy private individual.

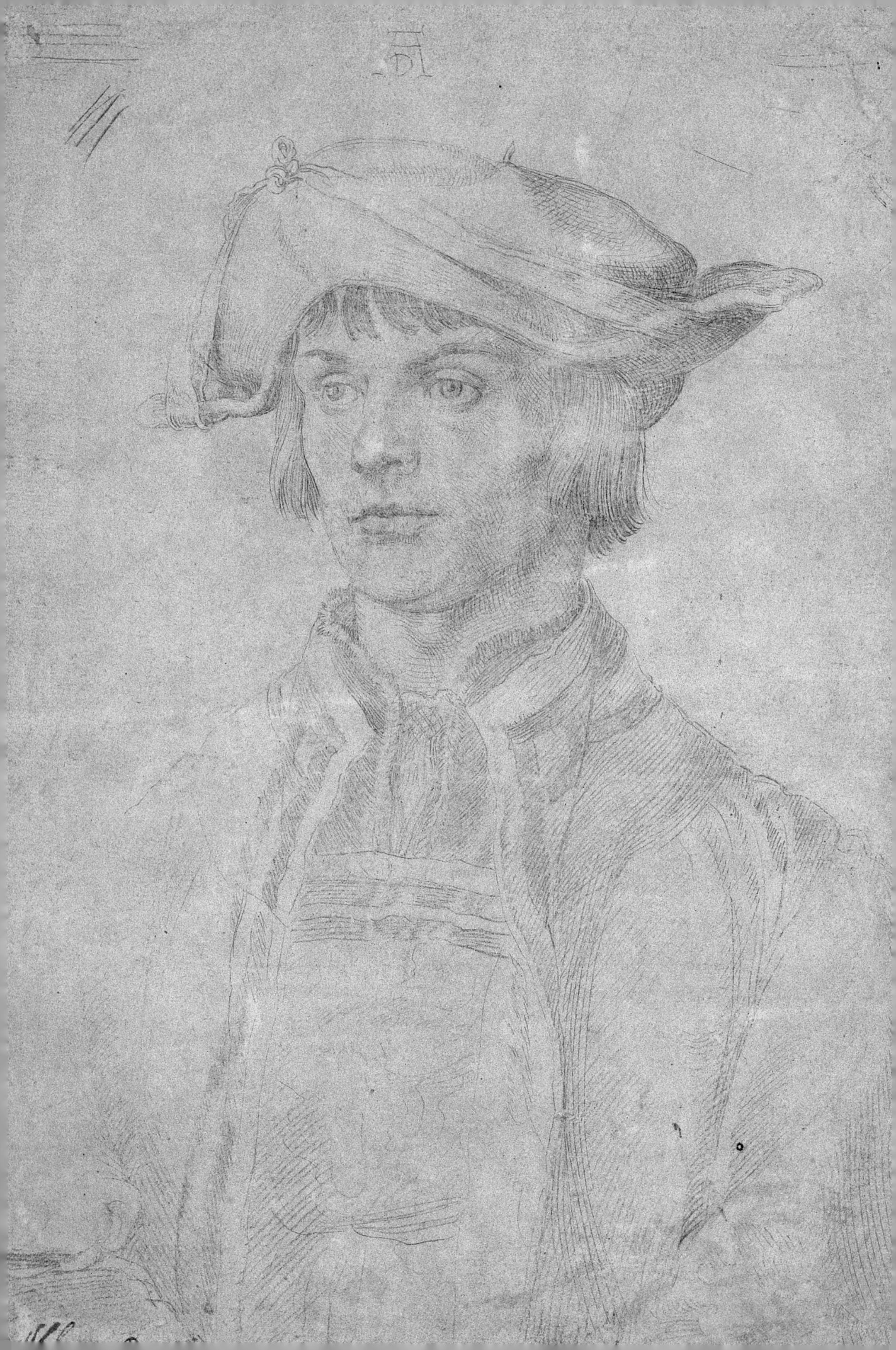

The life and work of Lucas van Leyden (1494-1533)

Lucas van Leyden is the most famous sixteenth-century Dutch painter, and it is no exaggeration to liken his significance to that of Rembrandt for seventeenth-century Dutch painting. That, in any event, was the view of the builders of the Rijksmuseum in 1884 when they depicted him as the representative of sixteenth-century painting alongside Rembrandt in a stained-glass window in the museum's entrance hall. The great flowering and versatility of seventeenth-century Dutch painting has tended to overshadow the preceding period, but that was not yet the case when Karel van Mander wrote the first history of northern Netherlandish painting of the fifteenth and sixteenth centuries, *Het Leven der Doorluchtighe Nederlandtsche, en Hooghduytsche Schilders* (The lives of the illustrious Netherlandish and German painters), which runs to more than 200 pages and was published in his *Schilder-boeck* of 1604.

9
Albrecht Dürer, *Portrait of Lucas van Leyden*, 1521. Silverpoint on prepared paper, 25.7 x 18 cm. Palais des Beaux-Arts, Lille. Dürer's diary shows that he met Lucas van Leyden in Antwerp in June 1521, that they exchanged prints, and that Dürer drew Lucas's portrait in silverpoint. This is believed to be that portrait, and it was engraved as such by Lampsonius as early as 1572.

VAN MANDER'S *SCHILDER-BOECK* AND OTHER SOURCES ON LUCAS VAN LEYDEN

Karel van Mander (1548-1606) was a southern Netherlandish artist who fled to Haarlem in 1585 for religious reasons, and worked there for the rest of his life as a creditable painter, draughtsman and print designer. His importance as a colleague and friend of Hendrick Goltzius and Cornelis Cornelisz van Haarlem is probably excelled by his standing as a writer about art. He wrote his book in imitation of the Italian painter Giorgio Vasari (1511-74), who in 1550 had written the lives of Italian architects, sculptors and painters. In the *Schilder-boeck*, Van Mander based his lives of Italian painters on Vasari's *Vite*, but he himself collected his information about Dutch and German painters, both past and present, from their fellow painters, relatives and collectors. Van Mander regarded Lucas van Leyden as the greatest Dutch painter of the sixteenth century, and he devoted as much space to him as he did to the Van Eyck brothers of the fifteenth century.
The pages on Lucas van Leyden are extremely informative. In addition to biographical details there is a résumé with brief descriptions of several of his engravings and paintings that were known to the author. Archival documents and other records generally confirm the accuracy of the biographical data supplied by him.

CHILD PRODIGY

According to Van Mander, Lucas van Leyden was born in May or June 1494 as the son of the painter Huygh Jacobsz. The archives show that he was one of the five children of Jacobsz and his first wife, Marie Hendriksdr, who must have died the year Lucas was born. Huygh Jacobsz (c. 1450-1535) is well documented in the archives, but unfortunately not a single work can

10
Albrecht Dürer, *The satyr's family*, 1505. Engraving, 11.5 x 7 cm. Rijksmuseum, Amsterdam. The elements that Lucas borrowed from this print are the composition, the positioning of the figures against a dark background, and the board with the engraver's monogram.

11
Lucas van Leyden, *Boy with a trumpet*, c. 1506. Engraving, 10.9 x 8.3 cm. Rijksmuseum, Amsterdam. A nude, seated boy, possibly a satyr, is playing a shawm to accompany the round dance of two children on the edge of a wood. The print has the same strange atmosphere as Dürer's *The satyr's family*. The nude figures and the engraving technique lack Dürer's perfection, but there is a refined interplay of light and shade that ties the figures to the space.

be attributed to him with any certainty. Van Mander describes Lucas as a child prodigy who 'seems to have been born with the art of painting and drawing, and with brush and burin in hand'. He took to art at an early age, and was already making engravings after his own designs at the age of nine. He made and sold his first painting when he was twelve. Van Mander states that he was taught by his father, who was 'an excellent painter in his time', before being apprenticed to the well-known Leiden artist Cornelis Engelbrechtsz.

LUCAS AS AN ENGRAVER

However, it was not his paintings that brought Lucas van Leyden his international fame but the 170 engravings that he made between around 1505 and 1530. It is not known who trained him as an engraver, of which there was no tradition in Leiden. Van Mander mentions an etcher of armour and a goldsmith as his teachers. Lucas must have been about ten years old when he started engraving. It seems likely that he, 'a master by nature' as Van Mander put it, was mainly self-taught as an engraver. He probably derived some of his technical skills from the art of glass engraving, which was a flourishing craft in Leiden at the time, and one that he must have practised himself. In addition, the engravings of Albrecht Dürer (1471-1528) (fig. 10), were undoubtedly his models and a source of inspiration from the very beginning. Lucas assimilated this influence and employed it in his own way in his earliest, undated small engravings (fig. 11). He also adopted Dürer's practice of signing his prints with his monogram, adding the letter L to almost all his engravings and

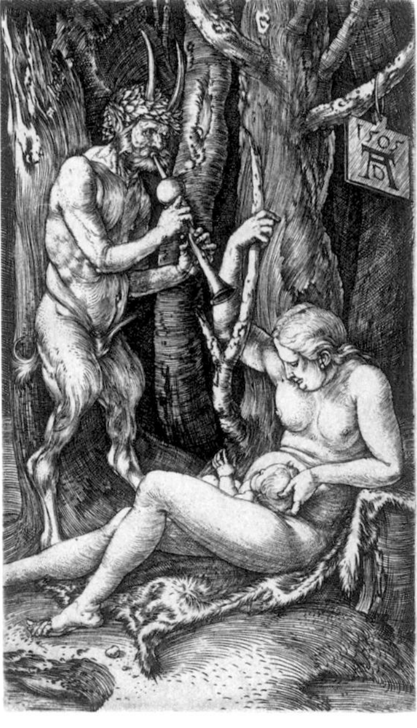

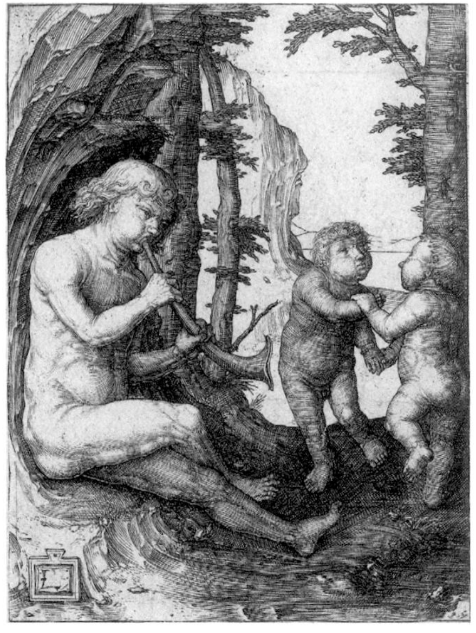

etchings. Albrecht Dürer can therefore be regarded as the young Lucas's teacher on paper. His earliest engravings, which can be dated between 1505 and 1508, show that he developed his own formal vocabulary and engraving style step by step, while his choice of narrative subjects was surprising and original.

Lucas's earliest dated engraving, *Mohammed and the monk Sergius* of 1508 (fig. 12), displays all the youthful mastery of the 14-year-old artist. It also demonstrates his skill as a storyteller. He chose an unusual, distinctive but rarely depicted moment from a story about the prophet. It is from one of the travel stories about the Holy Land by the fourteenth-century Jan van Mandeville. Mohammed meets the Christian hermit Sergius in the desert, and listens in fascination to his sermons until late at night. Irritated by this, Mohammed's servants decide to kill Sergius. One night, when Mohammed had drunk too much wine and had fallen asleep, the servants took his sword from its scabbard and killed the hermit. When Mohammed awoke from his stupor, his servants drew his attention to his bloodied sword, making him think that he had killed Sergius while drunk. Lucas depicts the moment when the deception is set in train. The dead Sergius lies stretched out on the ground with his throat cut. Sleeping beside him is the drunken prophet, leaning against a tree stump, while between them a servant is carefully placing the bloody sword beside Mohammed.

The speed with which the fame of Lucas's prints spread to Italy is demonstrated by a print of 1510 by the Italian engraver Marcantonio Raimondi after Michelangelo (fig. 13), in which the landscape was faithfully copied from Lucas's print of 1508. Lucas also showed himself to be a brilliant storyteller in his slightly later engravings, such as the large *Ecce homo* of 1510 (fig. 14). As in the engraving of Mohammed, the main event, in this case the presentation of Christ to the people, has been pushed back into the middleground. The people take centre stage in the foreground (as they do in the later triptych with *The dance around the golden calf*) in a wide variety of dress, poses and gestures. It is the people, not Pilate, who pass judgement on Christ, as it were. Everyday life is thus combined with a biblical event.

This is not the place to follow the fascinating development of Lucas van Leyden in his prints, but to show that even at an early age he had a totally individual style and narrative manner. There are dated prints from almost every year between 1508 and 1530 (with the exception of 1511, 1522 and 1526), and they enable us to trace his artistic and stylistic development from close at hand. Following the example of Albrecht Dürer, and in rivalry with him, Lucas built up a print oeuvre which is closer to the traditional iconography, in his Passion scenes among others, but which always remains remarkably original.

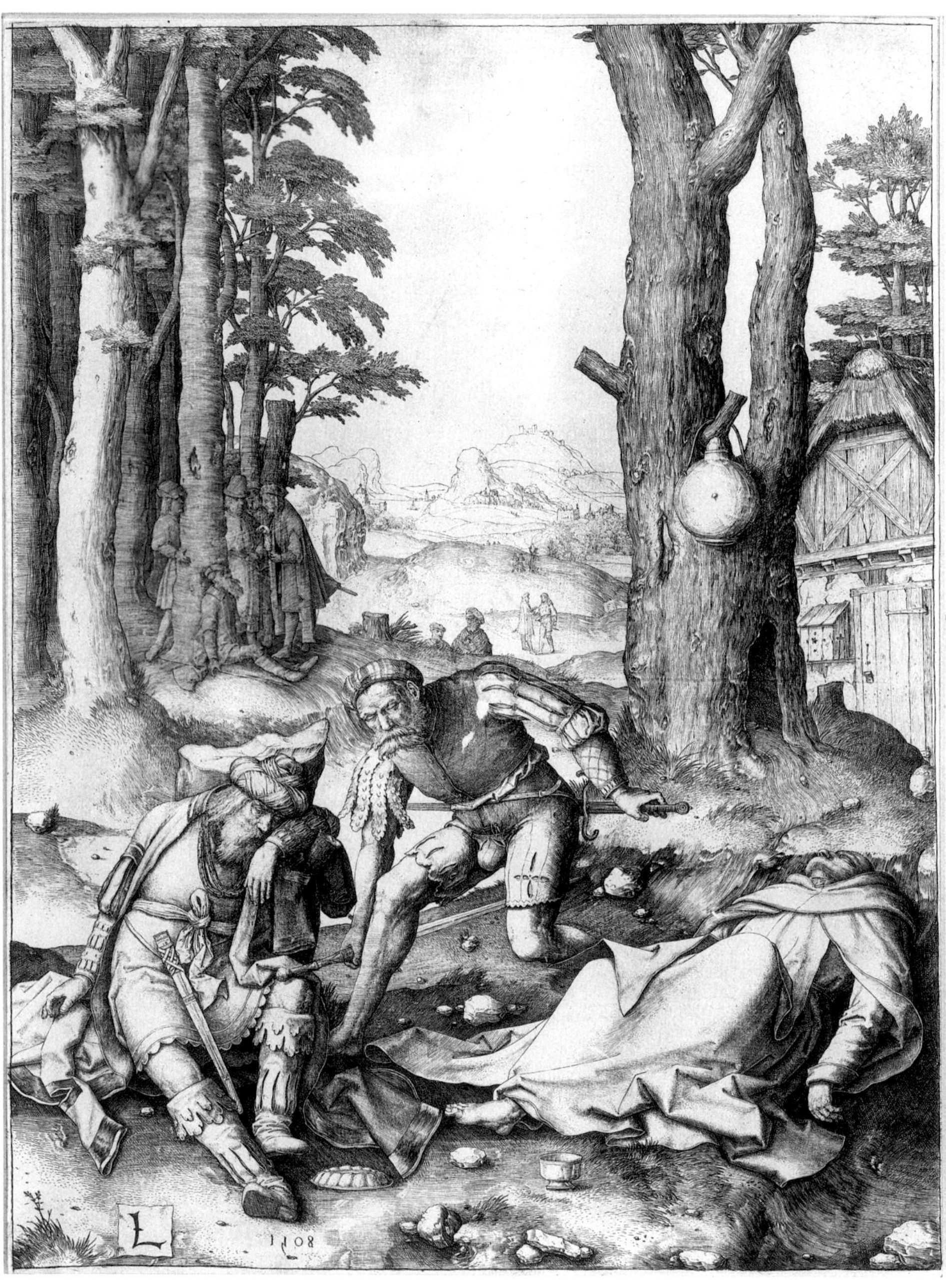

12
Lucas van Leyden, *Mohammed and the monk Sergius*, 1508. Engraving, 28.7 x 21.6 cm. Rijksmuseum, Amsterdam. This, Lucas's earliest dated engraving, which he must have made when he was 14 years old, shows the mastery he had acquired as an engraver in just a few years. He used an extremely refined engraving technique to achieve a convincing spatial structure with a natural recession into depth. He also managed to depict the most dramatic moment in the story in a credible way.

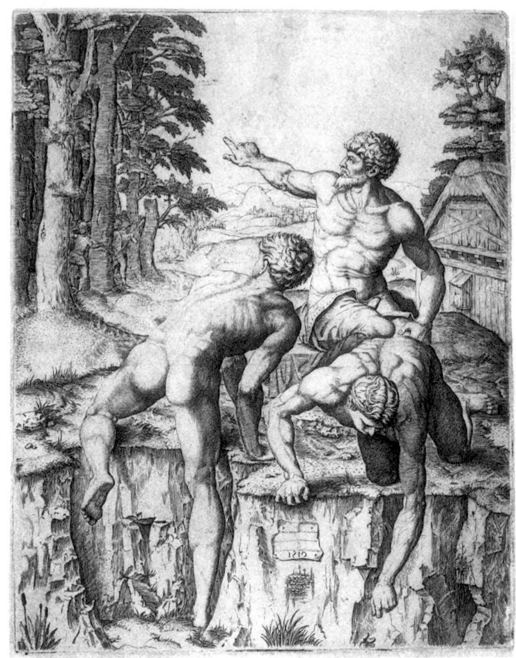

13
Marcantonio Raimondi after Michelangelo, *'The climbers', three nude men in a landscape*, 1510. Engraving, 28.8 x 22.8 cm. Rijksmuseum, Amsterdam. Lucas's work soon became known in Italy through his prints. The famous Italian engraver Raimondi here combined the background from Lucas's engraving of 1508 (fig. 12) with figures from a work of 1504-05 by the great Italian master Michelangelo.

14
Lucas van Leyden, *Ecce homo*, 1510. Engraving, 28.5 x 45.2 cm. Rijksmuseum, Amsterdam. This is one of the five engravings by Lucas van Leyden in large folio size, which became much sought after even during his lifetime.

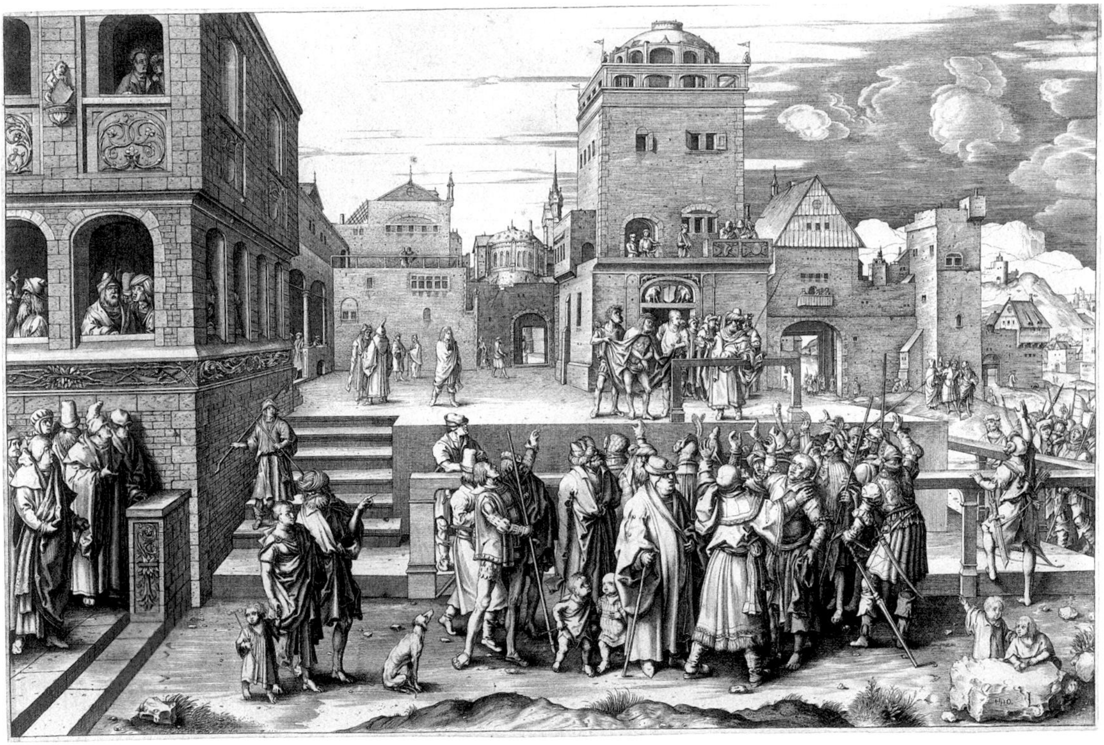

The early paintings

Lucas developed slightly later as a painter than he did as an engraver. As mentioned above, nothing is known about the paintings by his father, Huygh Jacobsz, and we have no way of telling how much he was shaped by him. More is known about the work of his second teacher, Cornelis Engelbrechtsz (c. 1462-1527), who supplied churches and monasteries in and around Leiden with altarpieces and devotional scenes produced in series with the aid of pupils and assistants. His colours are bright and his manner fairly broad. With the painting *Christ taking leave of his mother* of c. 1515-20, the Rijksmuseum has a fine, typical example of Engelbrechtsz's later, autograph work (fig. 15). Lucas van Leyden's paintings, only a few of which are known to have

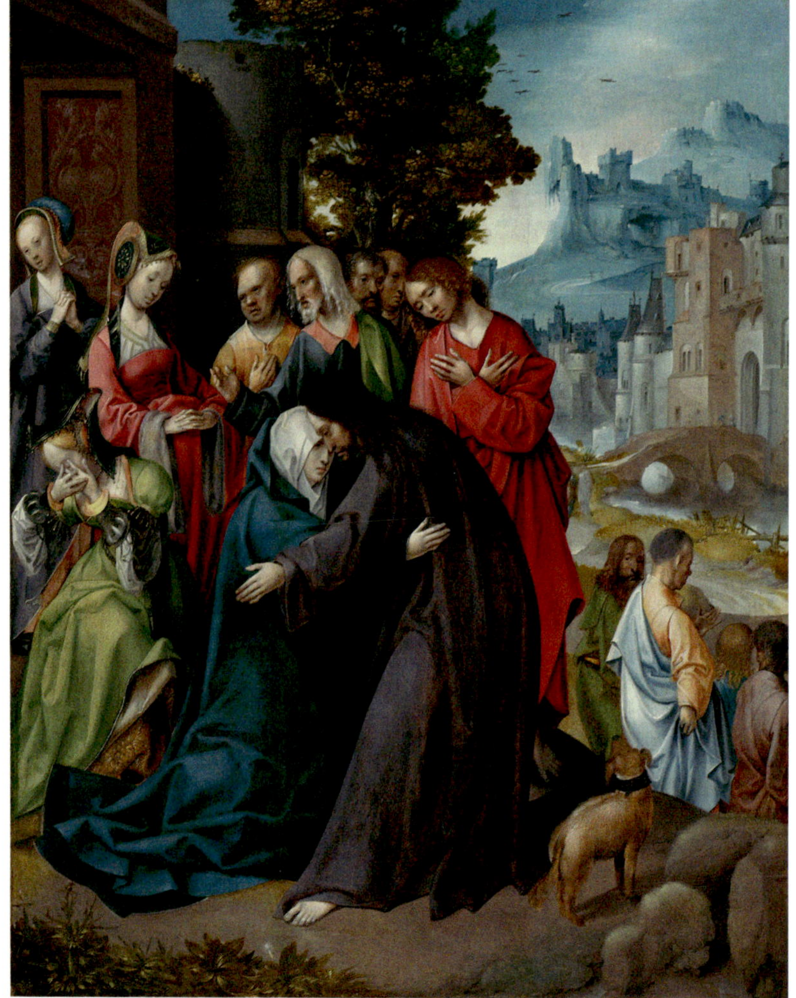

15
Cornelis Engelbrechtsz, *Christ taking leave of his mother*, c. 1515-20. Oil on panel, 54.7 x 44 cm. Rijksmuseum, Amsterdam. This panel, which must have been part of a larger group of scenes from the life of the Virgin, is a fine example of the mature work of Lucas's teacher. As in his pupil's work, the poses and gestures express the moving nature of this last meeting. The simple, warm colours of the figures contrast with the bright blue and white shapes in the rocky landscape background.

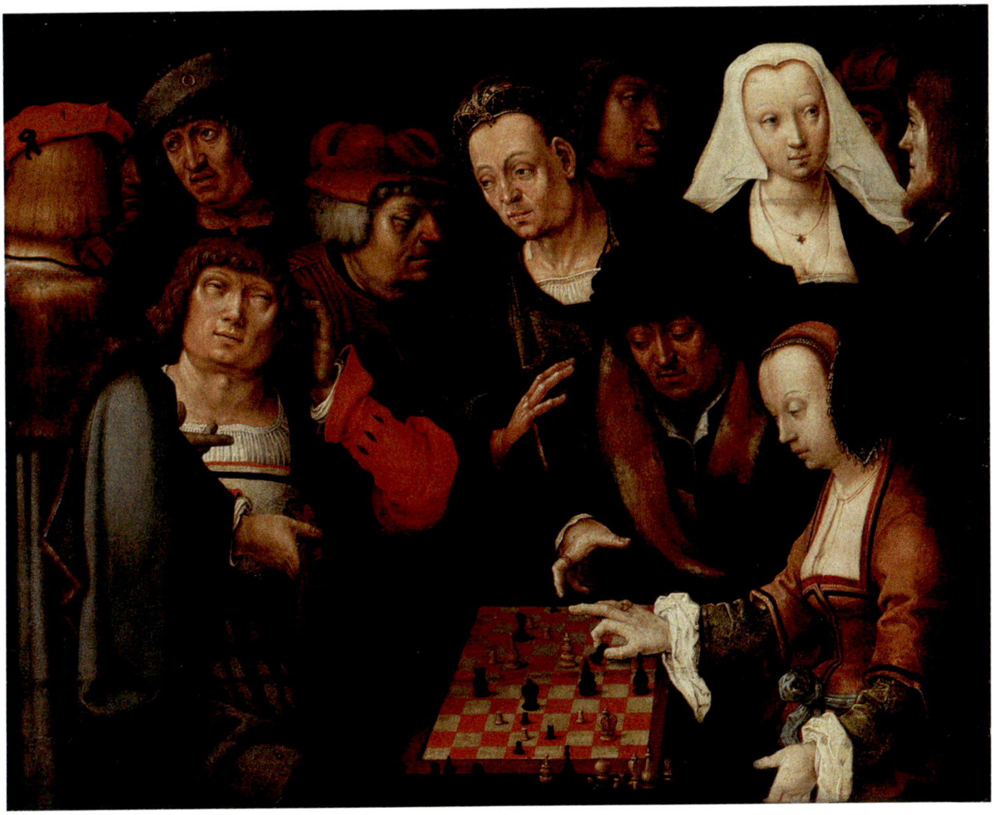

16
Lucas van Leyden, *Chess players*, c. 1508. Oil on panel, 26 x 36 cm. Gemäldegalerie, Staatliche Museen – Preussischer Kulturbesitz, Berlin. In the centre is a chessboard with 6 by 12 squares, with a young woman making a move on the advice of an older man, while her opponent leans back with his cap in his hand. One can only guess at the implications of what is happening, for the closely packed faces display little emotion.

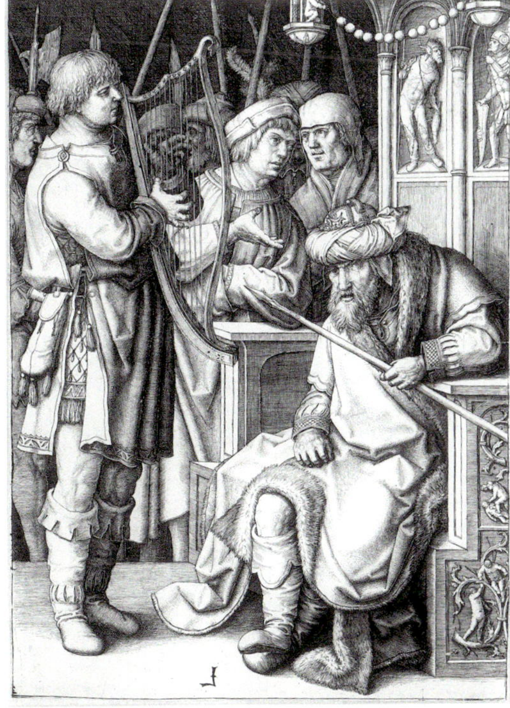

17
Lucas van Leyden, *David playing the harp for Saul*, c. 1508. Engraving, 25.2 x 18.2 cm. Rijksmuseum, Amsterdam. The spatial structure and formal vocabulary of this engraving are closely related to the painting *Chess players* (fig. 16), while the expression of rage on Saul's face can also be seen in the print with Potiphar's wife (fig. 18).

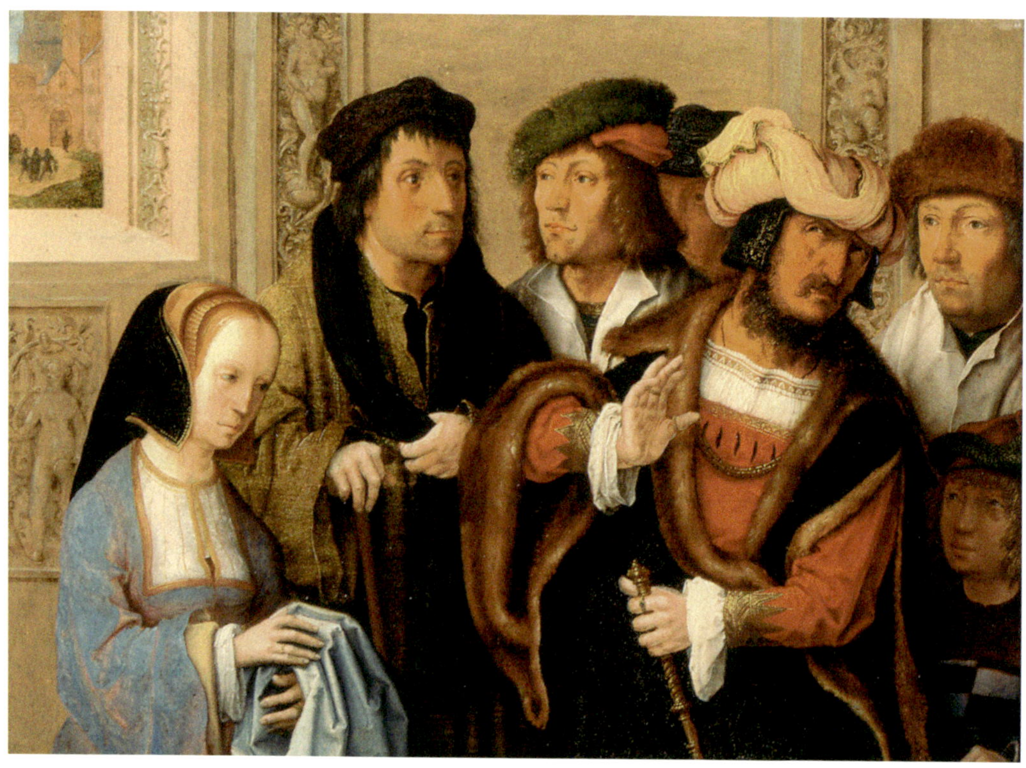

18
Lucas van Leyden, *Potiphar's wife showing her husband Joseph's cloak*, c. 1512. Oil on panel, 24 x 34.5 cm. Museum Boijmans Van Beuningen, Rotterdam. There is more space around the figures in this painting than in *Chess players* (fig. 16), and the colours are lighter, but the detailed, draughtsman-like manner of painting is very similar. The book of Exodus relates how Potiphar's wife had tried to seduce Joseph, her husband's servant and confidant. Joseph repulsed her advances and fled, leaving his cloak behind.

survived, are less conventional than Engelbrechtsz's traditional and frequently depicted religious subjects. As in the early prints, the subjects of most of Lucas's paintings are surprisingly original and the treatment innovative. His early work between 1508 and 1520 includes six half-length figure pieces with people playing chess or cards, Old Testament scenes, a few depictions of saints, and a Virgin and Child with angels. We will take a closer look at some of these here, while the larger later works will be discussed below in relation to *The dance around the golden calf*.

Lucas's earliest datable painting is probably *Chess players* (fig. 16), which is related to his engravings of the same period (fig. 17), in which there is almost no space around the figures, with the facial expressions seemingly being the main subject. The faces were drawn with a fine brush, and the costumes were modelled in saturated colours with numerous details.

A few years later, in Rotterdam, he painted *Potiphar's wife showing her husband Joseph's cloak* (fig. 18), in which the expressions on the faces, the gestures and poses evoke a subtle tension, while the draughtsmanship and colouring are highly refined.

Larger in size and thematically closer to the work of his contemporaries is *The Virgin and Child with angels* (fig. 19), in which Lucas makes great play of the Renaissance architecture and the ornamentation. The rich use of colour is now lighter in tone, but the execution

19
Lucas van Leyden, *The Virgin and Child with angels*, c. 1520. Oil on panel, 77.5 x 46 cm. Gemäldegalerie, Staatliche Museen – Preussischer Kulturbesitz, Berlin. The Virgin and Child and the angels are depicted in a traditional way in a carefully planned composition in which the ornate Renaissance architecture structures the space. The lavishness of the Renaissance ornamentation is reinforced by the lively use of colour. The vocabulary of forms is close to that in Lucas's engravings of the period, which were still heavily indebted to the work of Albrecht Dürer, who introduced him to the Renaissance style.

is as detailed and draughtsman-like as ever. In this painting, too, Lucas remains a graphic artist with an exceptionally good eye for colour. The painting can be dated around 1520, about the time that Lucas met Albrecht Dürer. It was only in the 1520s that he abandoned this fairly graphic manner as a painter, adopting instead a broader and more flowing touch.

THE MEETING WITH ALBRECHT DÜRER

Van Mander goes into some detail about the meeting between the two artists in his lives of both Albrecht Dürer and Lucas van Leyden. He thought that they had met in Leiden, but Dürer's diary shows that it took place in Antwerp in June 1521. The diary of his journey through the Netherlands, which he kept from July 1520 until July 1521, records what he did and saw, which artists he met, who had extended invitations to him, and the amounts for which he exchanged and sold prints. On 8 June 1521 he wrote: 'Master Lucas, who makes copper engravings, invited me as his guest. He is a small man, born in Leyden in Holland, and was in Antwerp. [...]
I drew the portrait of Master Lucas of Leyden in silverpoint' (fig. 9). He then noted: 'I exchanged prints with Lucas, his engravings for mine, to the value of 8 guilders'.
Lucas van Leyden's prints show how much he admired the German artist, and how he was an important model for him until the early 1520s. At the same time, though, they must have been competitors on the international market for prints, and in particular at the Frankfurt Buchmesse. In the years following their meeting, Dürer's hold on him waned and was replaced by a more agitated and vibrant formal vocabulary that betrays the influence of Jan Gossaert (c. 1478-1532). In the prints of 1528-30, in which nude figures play an important part, Lucas developed a new style closely allied to that of Italian prints. It was in that period that he made his large paintings, which will be discussed in the next chapter.

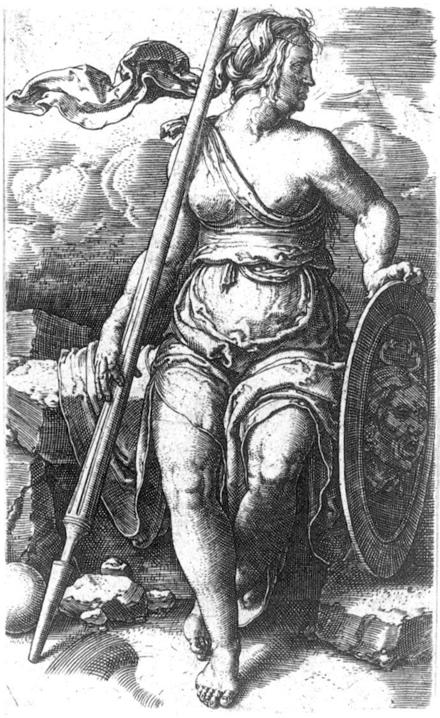

20
Lucas van Leyden, *Pallas Athena*, c. 1530. Engraving, 11.7 x 7 cm. Rijksmuseum, Amsterdam. Van Mander says that Lucas van Leyden worked on this engraving on his deathbed. It is closely connected to his late prints in the Italian manner. The engraving trials below the lance shows that the print was left unfinished. The monogram L was only added in that position later.

21
Detail of the landscape in the middleground of the right wing of *The dance around the golden calf.*

THE LATER LIFE OF LUCAS VAN LEYDEN

Lucas returned to Leiden soon after meeting Dürer, for at the end of June 1521 he had to stand surety for his brother Dirk, who was also a painter. He is documented in the city for the same purpose in 1525, and again in 1529. Little is known about his private life. Around 1510-12 he acknowledged a daughter, Maritge, who had been born out of wedlock. In 1515 he was still living in his father's house. Shortly after 1526 he married Lysbeth van Boshuysen, who was from a well-to-do Leiden family. Like his father, Cornelis Engelbrechtsz and his sons, Lucas was a member of the Crossbowmen's guild from 1514 to 1519. He received several major painting commissions in the second half of the 1520s. Unfortunately, there is no further documentary support for Van Mander's detailed account of a voyage by sea to Zeeland, Flanders and Brabant, in the course of which he met the painter Jan Gossaert in Middelburg. Since Van Mander says that Lucas was 33 at the time, this journey south must have taken place around 1527. Nor do we know anything more about the artist's subsequent debilitating illness than what is in the *Schilder-boeck*. In view of the large number of paintings and prints dated between 1526 and 1531, this must have been an extremely productive period, and it is difficult to imagine that he was away on a long voyage at the time. or was laid low by sickness. What is conceivable is that he was struck down in 1532-33, when there are no dated works. The engraving *Pallas Athena* (fig. 20), on which he worked while on his deathbed, is certainly unfinished, and was only given its L monogram later. This print of the patroness of the arts was a worthy crown on Lucas's career as an artist. He died in the summer of 1533, and was buried in the Church of St Peter in Leiden.

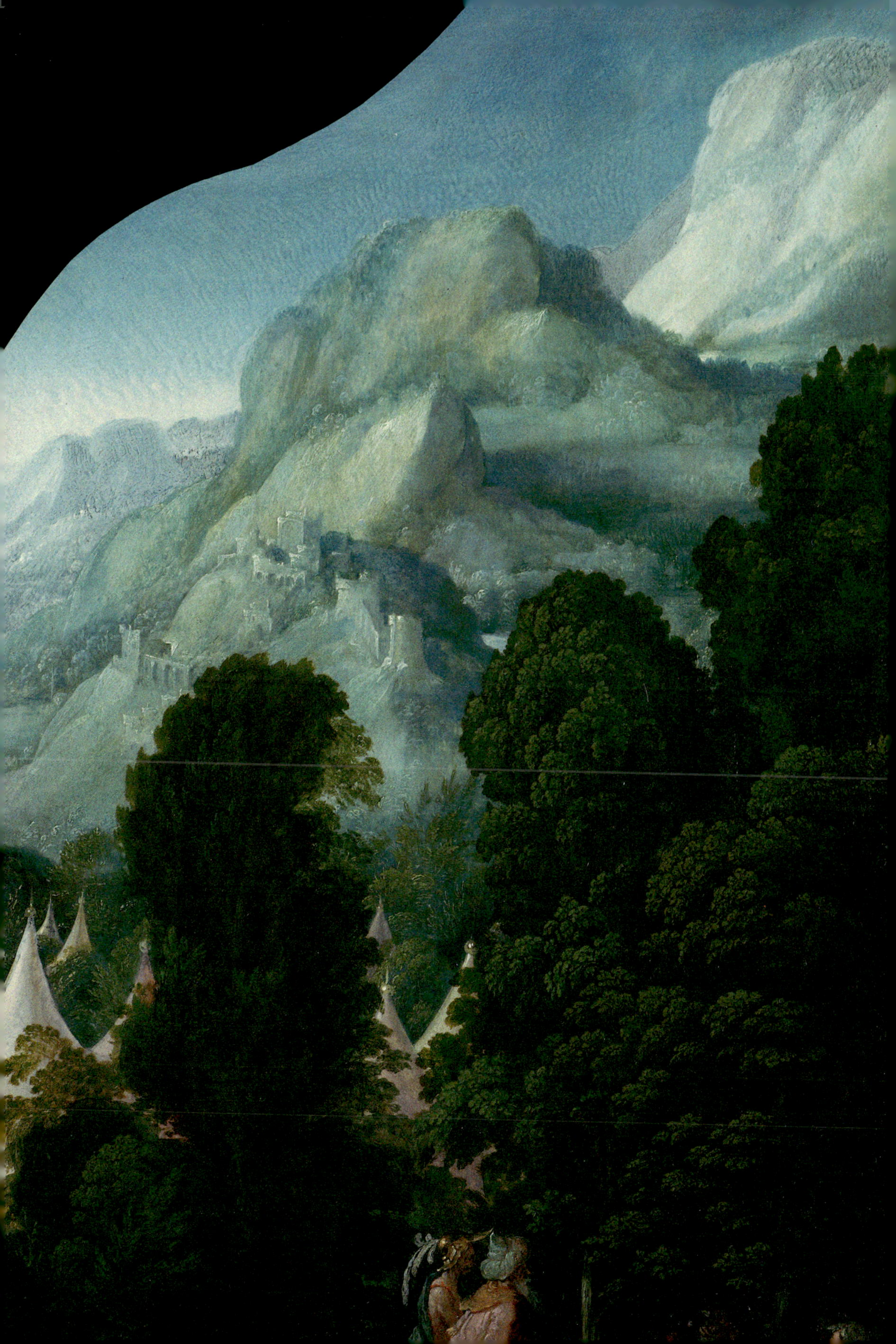

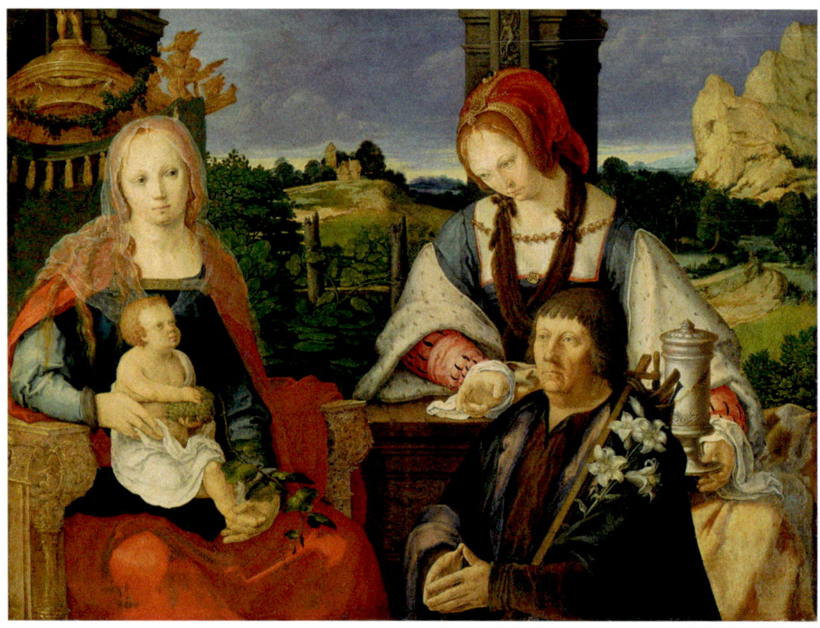

22
Lucas van Leyden, *The Virgin and Child, a donor and Mary Magdalen*, 1522. Oil on panel, 50.5 x 67.8 cm. Alte Pinakothek, Munich. This oblong panel is made up of two panels arched at the top which were originally the inner wings of a diptych. They were joined together on the orders of Elector Maximilian of Bavaria, who also had the painting considerably enlarged with the addition of a tall, Renaissance double archway (fig. 24). In addition to this overpainting, the praying donor was transformed into Joseph with the addition of his attributes of lilies and carpenter's tools.

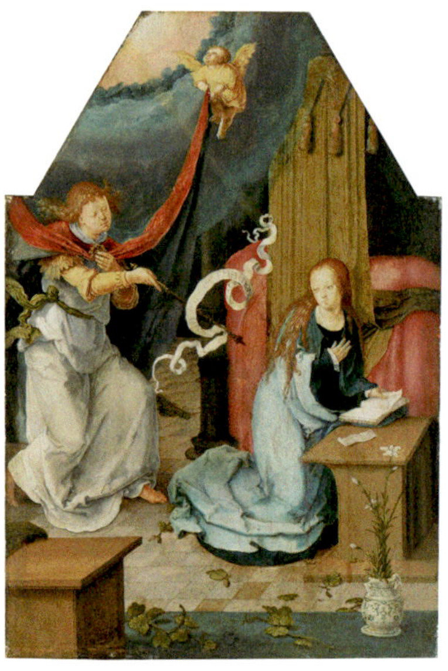

23
Lucas van Leyden, *The Annunciation*, 1522. Oil on panel, 42.2 x 29.2 cm. Alte Pinakothek, Munich. This scene, which was originally arched at the top, was revealed when fig. 22 was closed. It was on the back of the right wing, and was sawn off the composite panel in 1874. Some of the original paint layer was lost in the process, most notably in the Virgin's blue gown.

The late paintings

Remarkably, most of Lucas's paintings that Van Mander describes in his *Schilder-boeck* of 1604 have survived, and are still counted among his finest works. Van Mander knew that his paintings were few in number, but were 'pre-eminently worthy of admiration and very attractive on account of a certain special quality of an indefinable, attractive, appealing charm observable in them'. In addition to the description of *The dance around the golden calf* cited above (p. 5), Van Mander discusses three more paintings in the *Schilder-boeck*. They are all late works and are dated between 1522 and 1531. Lucas van Leyden's monumental works also include a large one of *Moses striking water from the rock*, executed

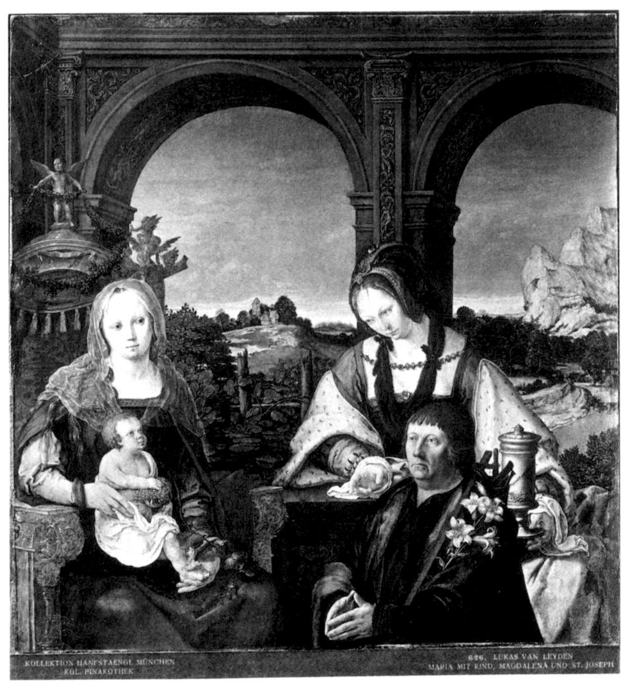

24
Lucas van Leyden, *The Virgin and Child, a donor and Mary Magdalen*, 1522, with the seventeenth-century additions. The painting before 1911. Alte Pinakothek, Munich. Like Emperor Rudolf II in Prague, Elector Maximilian I of Bavaria was an enthusiastic collector of works by Albrecht Dürer and his contemporaries. He would not tolerate any references to the original context and form of the paintings, ordering coats of arms, inscriptions and donors to be overpainted or removed, and 'beautified' the scenes with added landscapes and buildings in the Renaissance style. The section added to the top of the painting was removed in 1911, but the overpaint on the original part of the picture was left untouched.

in tempera on canvas, which has the monogram L and the date 1527 (fig. 27). Apart from the four works discussed in this book, only a few other panels from the period 1520-30 can be attributed to Lucas, among them a small Virgin and Child (fig. 63) and two male portraits.

THE VIRGIN AND CHILD, A DONOR AND MARY MAGDALEN (1522)

The panel with *The Virgin and Child, a donor and Mary Magdalen* (fig. 22) bears the monogram L and the date 1522. It was originally a diptych consisting of two panels arched at the top, with the Virgin and Child on the left wing and the donor being presented by Mary Magdalen on the right one, with *The Annunciation* painted on the outside (fig. 23). Van Mander describes it at length, and states that it belonged to Emperor Rudolf II in Prague. Around 1620, when it came into the possession of Elector Maximilian I of Bavaria, the two panels were joined together and extended considerably at the top (fig. 24). The praying donor was transformed into Joseph by the addition of a staff and lilies. *The Annunciation* was sawn off in 1874 so that it could be exhibited on its own. Most of the additions to the top of the large panel were removed in 1911. This panel with the joined inner wings of the triptych is now on display in the Alte Pinakothek in Munich, alongside *The Annunciation*. Despite the alterations and additions (parts of the canopy, the pillar and the donor in the guise of Joseph), the panel is a superb example of Lucas's extremely refined and lively manner of painting. The bunch of grapes in the Christ Child's hand is a reference to the Passion and the Eucharist. This association is echoed by the vine leaves in the foreground of *The Annunciation*, which was originally the outside of the diptych. Interestingly, those outer wings are painted far more loosely and broadly than the inner ones. The figure types and ornamentation of the inner wings still display the influence of Albrecht Dürer, whom Lucas had met shortly before in Antwerp.

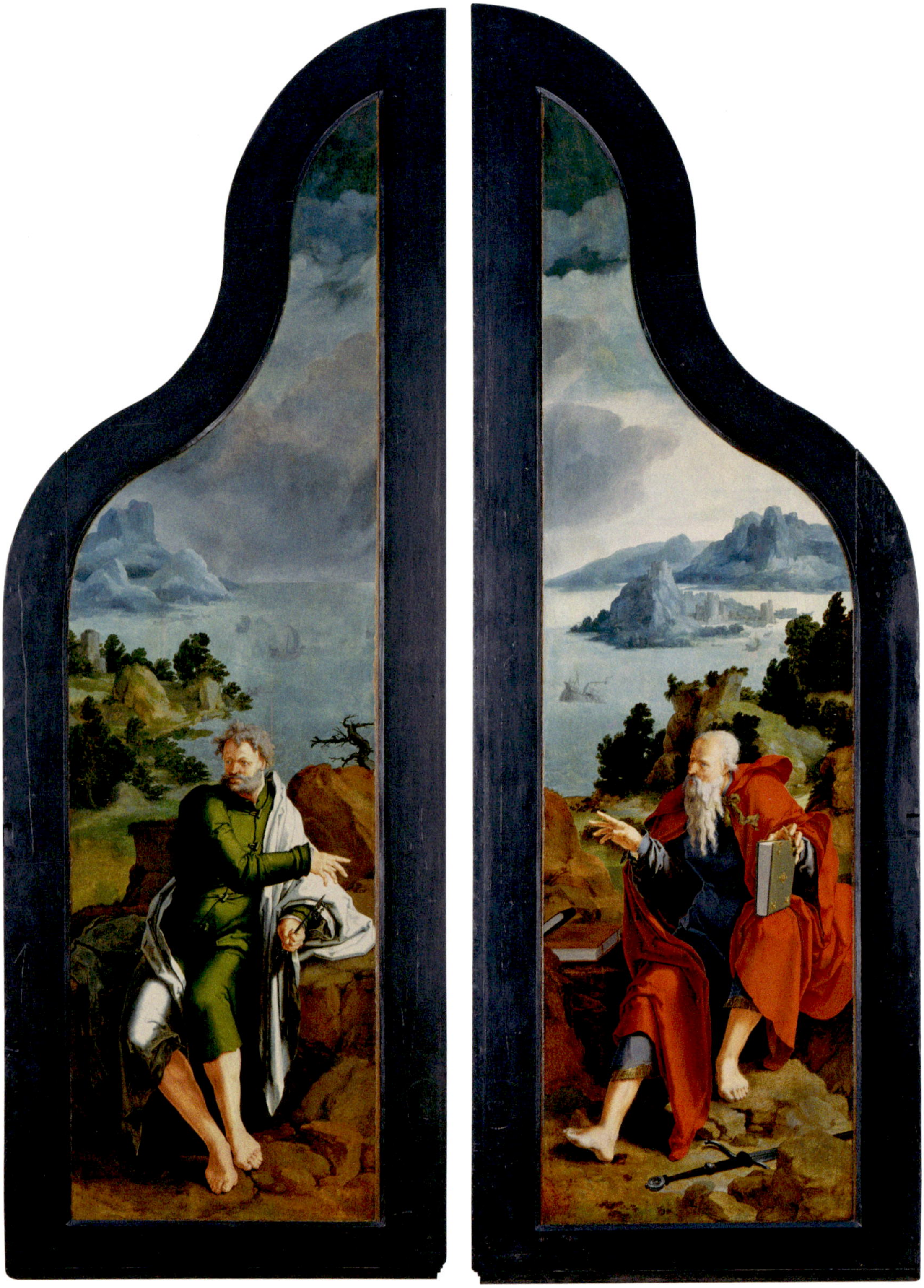

25
Lucas van Leyden, outer wings of fig. 26, *Sts Peter and Paul*, 1526-27. Oil on panel, including the frame, 300.5 x 217 cm. Stedelijk Museum De Lakenhal, Leiden. On the outer wings of the triptych, which are still in their original frames, are the apostles Peter and Paul, the patron saints of the city of Leiden. Their poses and gestures make it clear that Peter with the key and Paul with a sword and book are in conversation. The two panels are linked by the broad landscape.

TRIPTYCH WITH THE LAST JUDGEMENT (1526-27)

Lucas van Leyden's largest work is the *Triptych with the Last Judgement* (fig. 26), with *Sts Peter and Paul* on the outer wings (fig. 25), which is in the Stedelijk Museum De Lakenhal in Leiden. The triptych was an epitaph to the memory of Claes Dircksz van Swieten, timber merchant, civic magistrate and member of the Leiden city council, who died in 1525. The Van Swieten family awarded the commission to Lucas on 26 August 1526 for the sum of 35 Flemish pounds, or 200 guilders. He delivered the painting before the end of 1527, and it was installed near the font in Leiden's Church of St Peter. The family took the triptych away for safekeeping during the Iconoclasm of 1566, and in 1577 it was hung in the burgomasters' chamber in the town hall. Van Mander also mentions the story, known from other sources, that Emperor Rudolf II tried in vain to buy it for an astronomical sum.

Van Mander praised the draughtsmanship and the colouring of the nude figures, but felt that 'they have a little too much contrast on the bright side, and are too abruptly cut off'. He clearly preferred the outer wings with Sts Peter and Paul, which he considered to be far finer and more flowing, with greater care taken over the draperies and the landscape around the apostles. While the colours are saturated on the outer wings, and the figures and landscape form a superb whole, the light, radiant inner wings with the numerous nudes and the flamboyant scene of hell are a convincing demonstration of Lucas's ability to apply a northern vocabulary to Italian Renaissance art.

MOSES STRIKING WATER FROM THE ROCK (1527)

In 1527, the same year as the *Triptych with the Last Judgement*, Lucas painted his canvas *Moses striking water from the rock* (fig. 27). It is not mentioned by Van Mander, who instead discusses an *Adoration of the Magi* in watercolour on canvas, which is now lost. Although many paintings were made using this technique in the Low Countries, they were so fragile that few have survived. This is one of the finest examples. It shows Moses and the people of Israel shortly after he had struck a spring of water from a rock (Exodus 17:1-7; see p. 7). Men, women and children in the foreground are drinking water, carrying casks and pitchers, and conversing. On the right, lavishly attired, stand Moses and his brother Aaron. The surface is matte as a result of the tempera and watercolour technique with which the paint was applied, and the fine canvas, but the drawing is very rich, and in its details it is closely related to the other late paintings. The way in which the people are depicted is very reminiscent of *The healing of the blind man of Jericho* (fig. 28) and of *The dance around the golden calf*, although there the figures are far smaller.

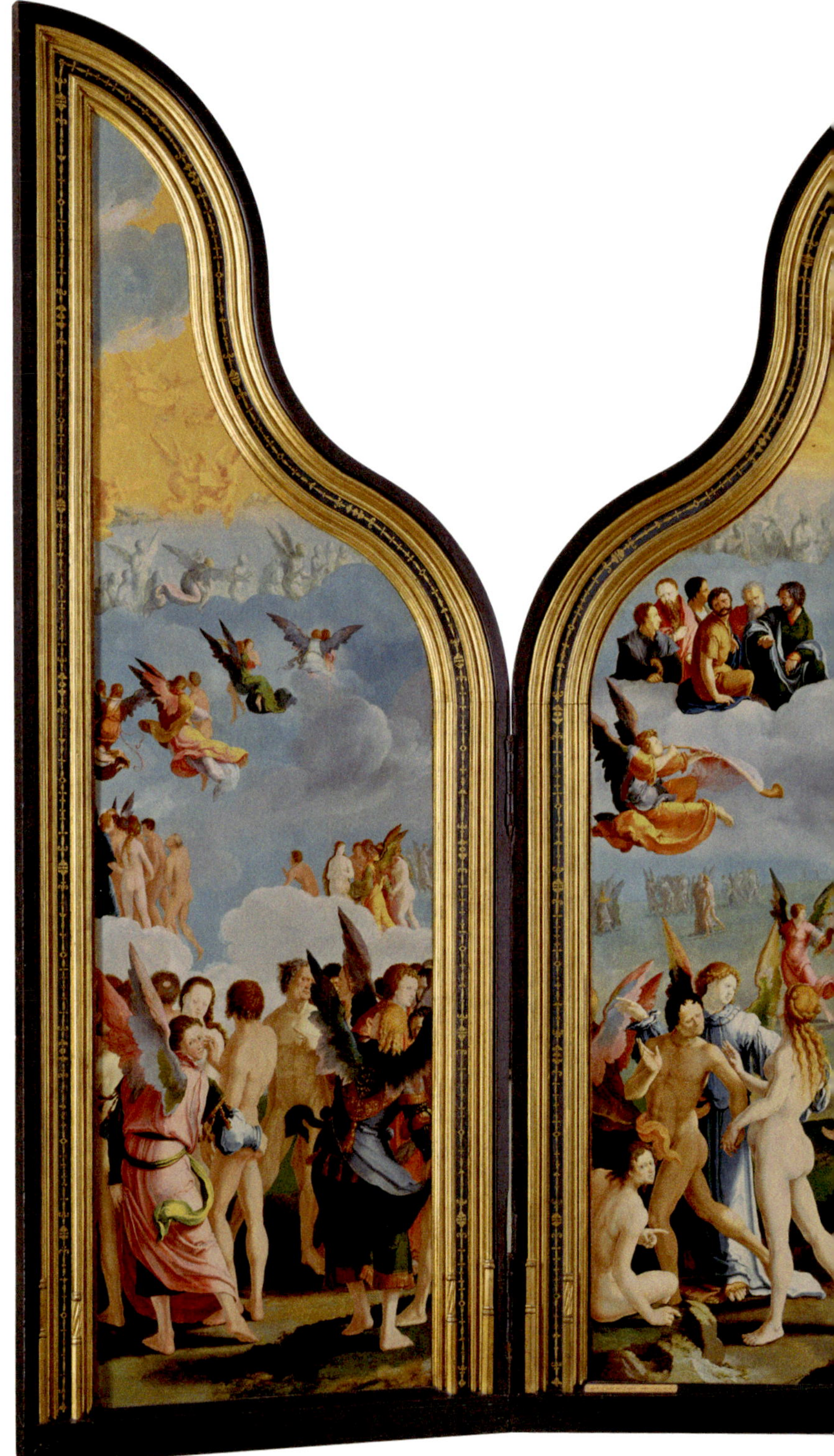

26
Lucas van Leyden, *Triptych with the Last Judgement*, 1526-27. Oil on panel, including the frame, 300.5 x 217 cm. Stedelijk Museum De Lakenhal, Leiden. In 1577 this triptych was installed in the burgomasters' chamber of Leiden town hall, along with two triptychs by Cornelis Engelbrechtsz. As a scene of the dispensation of justice, it remained acceptable to the city administration, which was now Protestant, although around 1600 the figure of God was painted over and replaced with the Hebrew letters for Yahweh. Travel guides show that the triptychs were tourist attractions. They were put on display in the Stedelijk Museum De Lakenhal when it opened in 1872. *The Last Judgement* is one of the focal points of the museum's collection, and is exhibited in such a way that the fronts and backs of the panels can be seen.

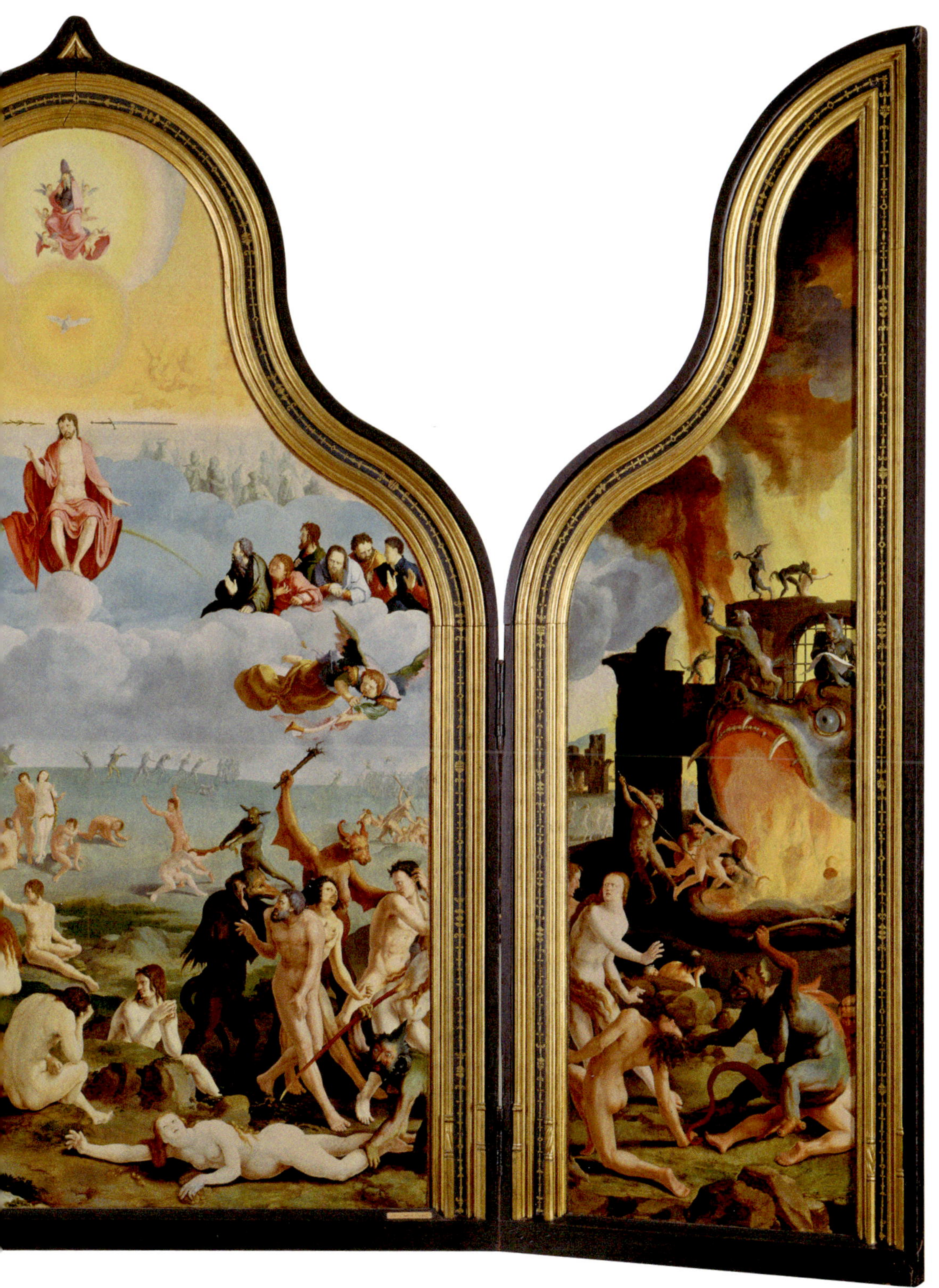

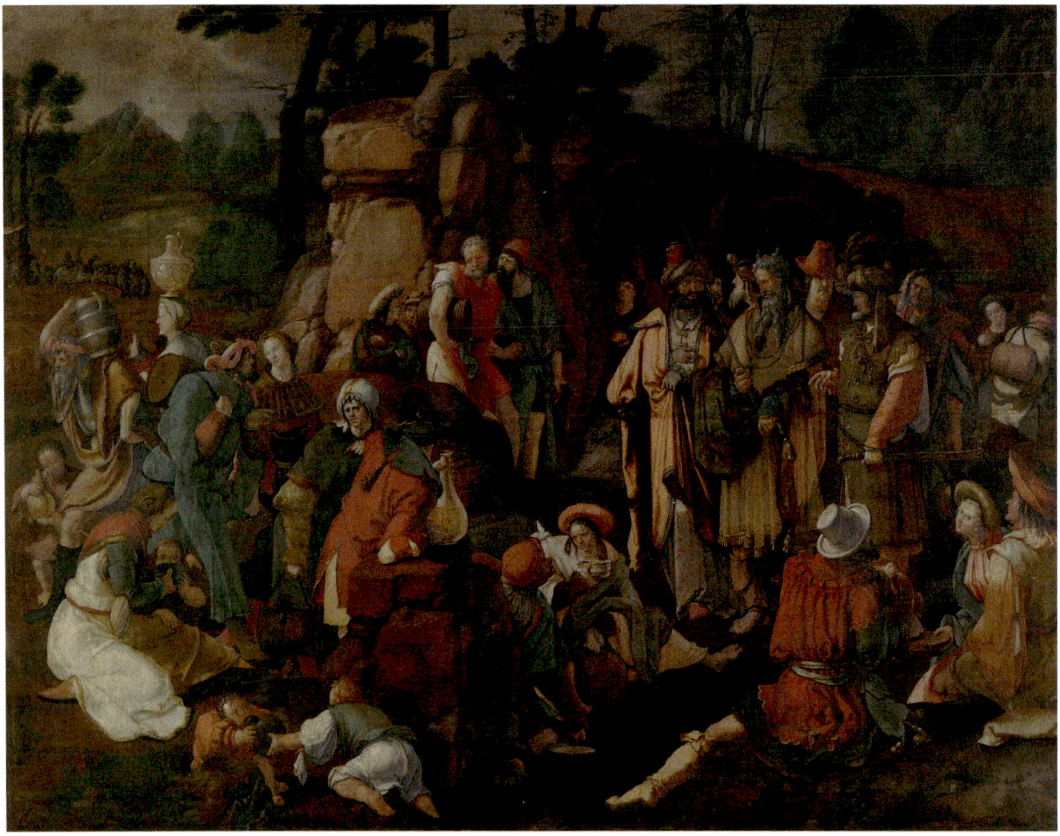

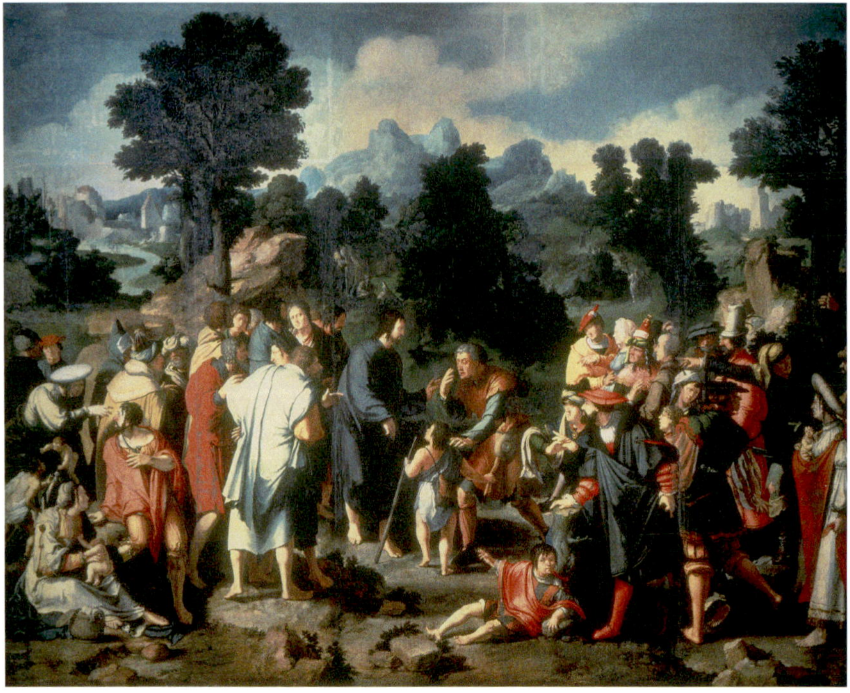

27
Lucas van Leyden, *Moses striking water from the rock*, 1527. Tempera on canvas, 183 x 118.5 cm. Museum of Fine Arts, Boston, William B. Richardson Fund. The painting was already recognised as a work by Lucas van Leyden when it was in the Borghese Collection in Rome in the seventeenth century. It was bought by the Germanisches Nationalmuseum in Nuremberg in 1900, which sold it after the Second World War because it no longer fitted within the museum's policy of concentrating on German art. It was on loan to the Rijksmuseum in 1952, and was bought by the Museum of Fine Arts in 1954.

28
Lucas van Leyden, *The healing of the blind man of Jericho*, 1531. Originally a triptych, oil on panel, transferred from panel and joined together on canvas, 115.7 x 150.3 cm. Hermitage, St Petersburg. The wings must have been sawn through in the mid-eighteenth century, when the painting was in a French collection. In order to make the combined composition rectangular it was necessary to paint in an extra part of the landscape and the sky at the top. After the conjoined insides and outsides of the triptych were acquired by the Russian Empress Catherine II in 1772, the painting was transferred to canvas, with the added sections at the top being preserved.

THE HEALING OF THE BLIND MAN OF JERICHO (1531)

Van Mander believed that Lucas van Leyden's very best and most beautiful work was a triptych with *The healing of the blind man of Jericho*, which used to bear the date 1531 (fig. 28). The coats of arms with male and female supporters painted on the outer wings identify the donors as the patrician couple Jacob van Montfoort Florisz and Dirckgen Dirck Boelensdr, also called Van Lindenburgh. The triptych was most likely an epitaph to their memory. In 1604 it belonged to Van Mander's friend, the painter Hendrick Goltzius, who probably bought the triptych from the donors' heirs after it had lost its ecclesiastical function after the Iconoclasm and the Reformation. Emperor Rudolf II also made a vain attempt to acquire this triptych for his collection in Prague. *The healing of the blind man of Jericho* is another painting that is not in its original form. The backs of the wings were separated from the fronts in the mid-eighteenth century, and the scene originally covering the wings and the centre panel was turned into a single painting, with additions. The tops of the panels with the coats of arms, which probably bore the date 1531, must have been lost when this was done. The painting was transferred to canvas in the Hermitage in the nineteenth century, and it can be seen there today. The original centre panel depicts the moment preceding the healing

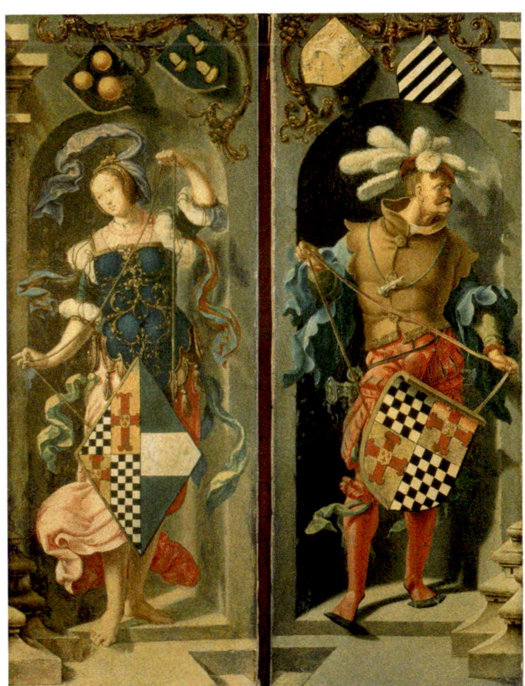

29
Lucas van Leyden, *Supporters with the coats of arms of the Van Montfoort family*, 1531. The original outer wings of fig. 28, transferred from panel and joined together on canvas, 89 x 70 cm. Hermitage, St Petersburg. The panels with the elegant supporters and the donors' arms must have been sawn down at the top to make them rectangular, and it was then that the date 1631 mentioned by Van Mander would have been lost.

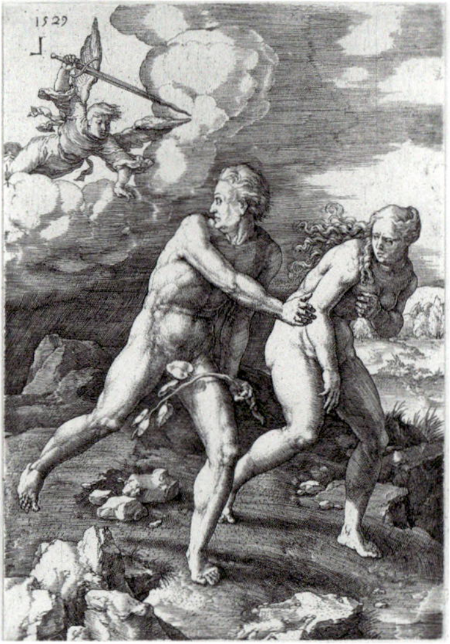

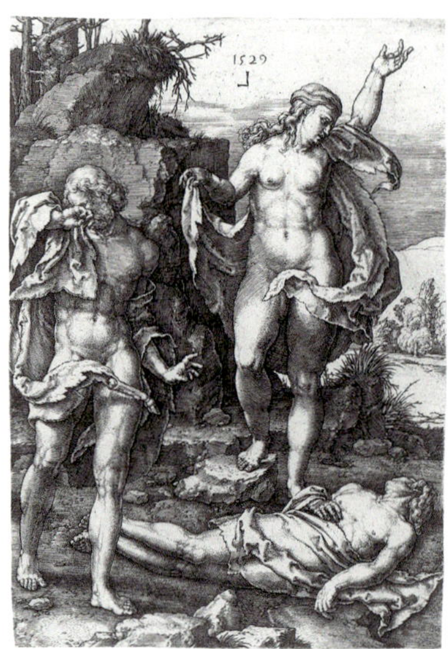

30 a-b
Lucas van Leyden, two prints from the series *The story of Adam and Eve*, 1529: a) *The expulsion from Paradise*, b) *Adam and Eve mourning the dead Abel*. Engravings, approx. 16.2 x 11.5 cm each. Rijksmuseum, Amsterdam. The prints show nude human bodies in a variety of poses, actions and emotions closely allied to the landscape in which they are placed.

of the blind Bartimaeus in Jericho, as described in Mark 10:46-52. The blind man, supported by a young companion, approaches Christ. His healing is an exemplum of true faith, for the blind man has recognised the Messiah. In the foreground are the disciples, the unbelieving scribes, and onlookers. The background landscape, which originally extended across all three panels, is a broad panorama with trees, mountains and two cities, which can be taken to be Jerusalem and Jericho. The green landscape recalls the one on the outer wings of *The Last Judgement* (fig. 25) and in *The dance around the golden calf* (fig. 21). As a result of its treatment in the past, with the fronts and backs of the wings being separated, and the

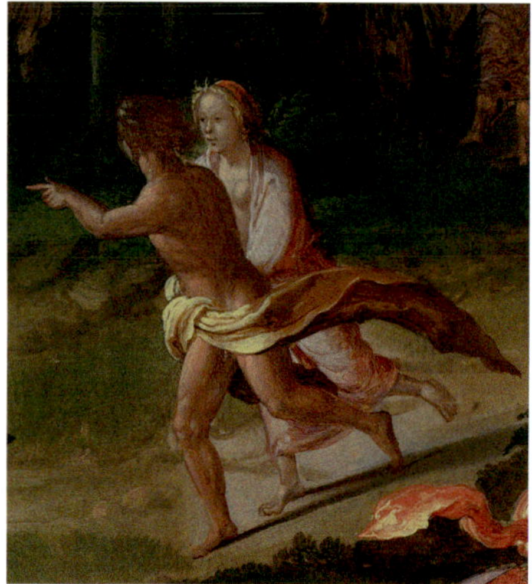

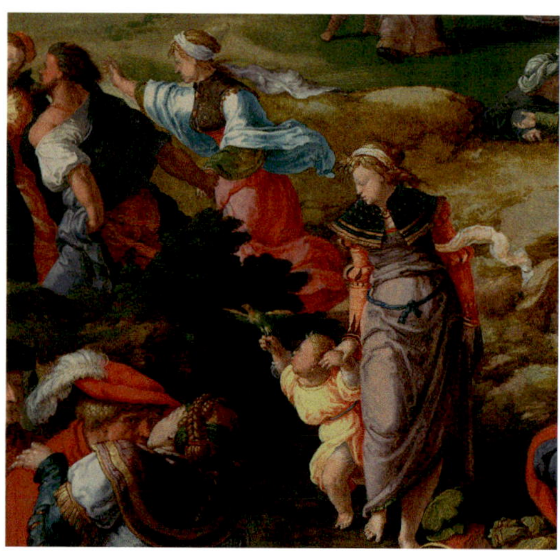

31 a-b
Details from *The dance around the golden calf*: a) centre panel, a couple running, b) detail of the right wing.

transfer to canvas, the painted surface is not nearly as well preserved as that of *The dance*.

Despite the obvious differences in the scale of the figures, *The healing of the blind man of Jericho* of 1531 displays the most similarities to *The dance around the golden calf* as regards the types of figure, use of colour and the landscape, so the latter can be dated around the same time, c. 1530. As regards the dating, it is worth taking a look at Lucas's engravings of the period. In 1528 he introduced a new style in his engraved work modelled on Italian examples, in which idealised nudes play a leading role. A pinnacle in this development is the 1529 series of six engravings with *The story of Adam and Eve* (fig. 30 a-b). There are many similarities between the figures in *The dance* and those in this series, and the engravings contain specimens of figures in motion that are also found in *The dance* (fig. 31 a-b).

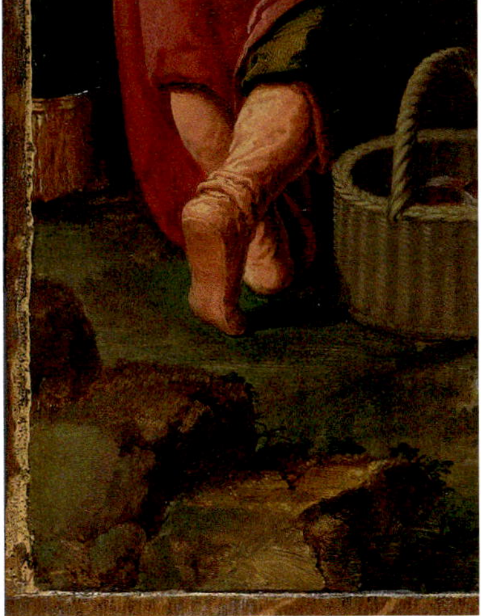

32
Detail of the left side of the left wing of *The dance around the golden calf* showing the unpainted edge and the barbe.

The genesis of *The dance around the golden calf*

In the fifteenth and early sixteenth centuries, a frame and the panel on which a scene was to be painted formed a single unit. It was not the painter but a cabinetmaker or carpenter who made the panel and the frame in which it was placed. Before the painter began applying the underdrawing and the paint layers, both the frame and the panel were covered with a layer of white ground consisting of chalk and glue. The painting was built up with several paint layers on this ground, and the frame was gilded and painted. That was also the case with this triptych, the original frame of which had already been removed and replaced with another one early in the seventeenth century. The centre panel consists of two vertical oak planks of equal width which are 0.5 cm thick at the edges and 1.3 cm thick in the middle, where they were glued together with the aid of a mortise and tenon joint and two horizontal dowels (fig. 33). Each of the wings is a single plank some 0.9 cm thick. It can be seen from the unpainted edges around the three panels that they were painted while they were in their frames (figs. 32, 33). Beside the unpainted edge, which is a strip of bare wood that was covered by the frame, there is a raised ridge of paint, the barbe, that connects the frame with the panel. In most cases this barbe broke off long ago due to the wood shrinking, even

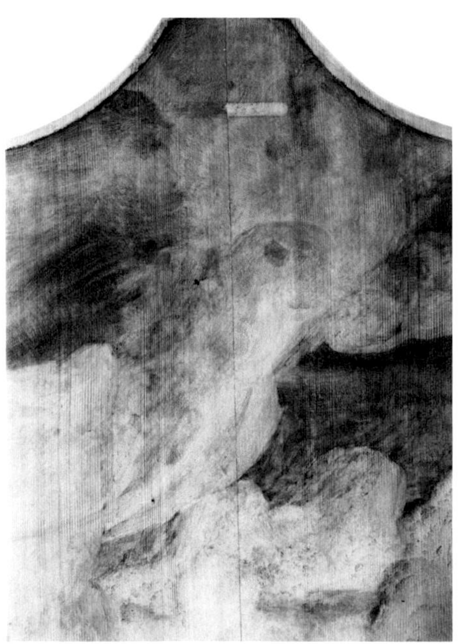

33
x-ray photograph of the top of the centre panel of *The dance around the golden calf*. The raised barbe along the unpainted edge at the top shows up as a white line. In the middle is the join between the two planks of the panel, and a little lower down the horizontal mortise and tenon joint, which is approx. 8 cm long (the dowel has broken off, leaving only the left half).

in paintings that are still in their original frames. The presence of unpainted edges with barbes on all three panels shows that the entire painted surface has survived.

DATING THE PANELS

The only wood used for panels (and frames) in the Netherlands at the time of this triptych was oak, which came from the Baltic region: present-day Poland, Estonia, Latvia and Lithuania. Thanks to the development of dendrochronological research in recent decades it is possible, using a magnifying glass, to count and measure the annual rings in planks, and to determine which is the youngest heartwood ring. From this one can deduce the earliest possible felling date of the tree, and the year after which the panel could have been painted. However, one can never date a painting on the basis of this information alone. It does provide a *terminus post quem*, the earliest possible date when the panel could have been painted, but that could also have been done much later. Dendrochronological examination of the centre panel shows that its youngest heartwood ring was formed in 1507, which means that the wood could not have been used to make a panel before 1518. However, when the time needed for the wood to dry and other factors are taken into account the date when the panel was used would have been at least 20 to 25 years after the date of the youngest heartwood ring, around 1530, in other words, which confirms the dating of the triptych on stylistic grounds.

EXAMINING THE UNDERDRAWING

In the case of fifteenth and sixteenth-century panel paintings, it was usual for the artist to draw the composition with chalk, charcoal or a brush on the white ground. That drawing, which was sometimes extremely detailed but could also be very sketchy, is called the underdrawing. Parts of it can sometimes be seen with the naked eye through a paint layer that has become transparent, particularly in white and red passages. With the aid of infrared reflectography, a method developed in the late 1960s by professor J.R.J. van Asperen de Boer, it has become possible in many cases to see

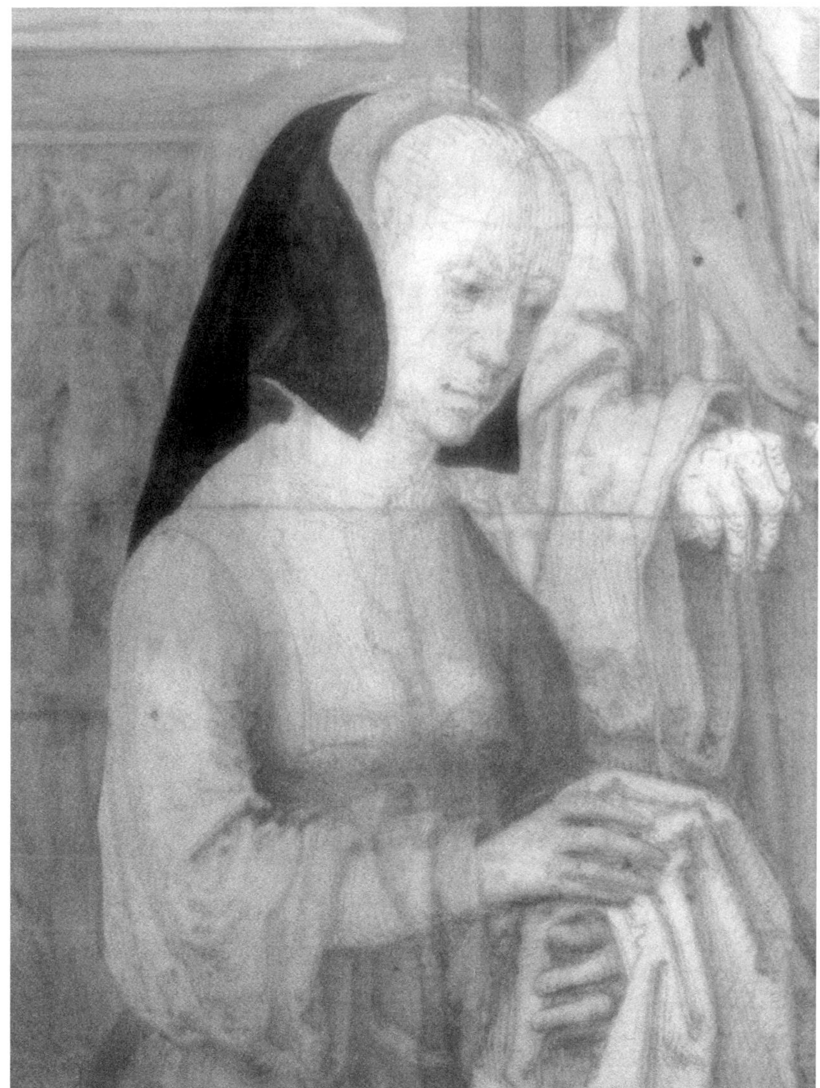

34
Infrared reflectogram assembly (IRR assembly) of the underdrawing of the lower left section of *Potiphar's wife showing her husband Joseph's cloak* (fig. 18). The very precise drawing was applied with a fine brush and black paint. The contours and the modelling of the face were drawn with flowing lines. It can be seen that the artist originally planned a veil over the forehead of Potiphar's wife. Her fingers are indicated with fine hatchings, as are the shaded areas of her dress.

all or most of the underdrawing. This cannot be done if the drawing was made with red chalk or brown bistre, or if it is under black paint or a very thick layer of paint. But if it was drawn with a medium containing a black pigment, the photographs of the underdrawing, which are known as infrared reflectogram assemblies, make it possible to analyse the part played by the underdrawing in the creation of the finished picture. By describing the individual characteristics of the underdrawing it is possible to lend added weight to an attribution to a particular master.

35
IRR assembly of the washed underdrawing of the figure group in the left foreground of the centre panel of the *Triptych with the Last Judgement* (fig. 26).

36
IRR assembly of the underdrawing in the group of the chosen ones in the middleground of the centre panel of the *Triptych with the Last Judgement* (fig. 26). The figures were first drawn with a brush, with the shaded passages indicated with broad strokes. In the underdrawing the young man first had his hands and head raised, but in the painted surface he is looking down. The changes are indicated with chalk.

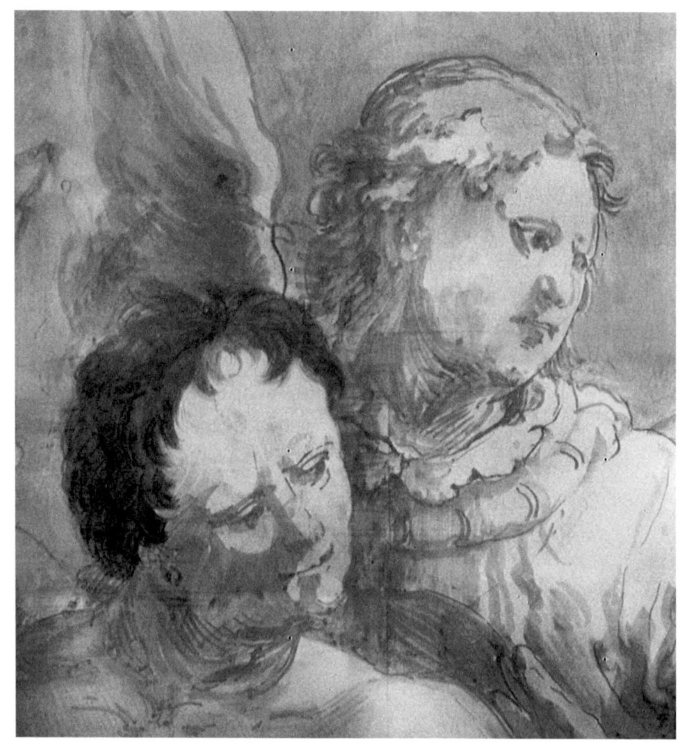

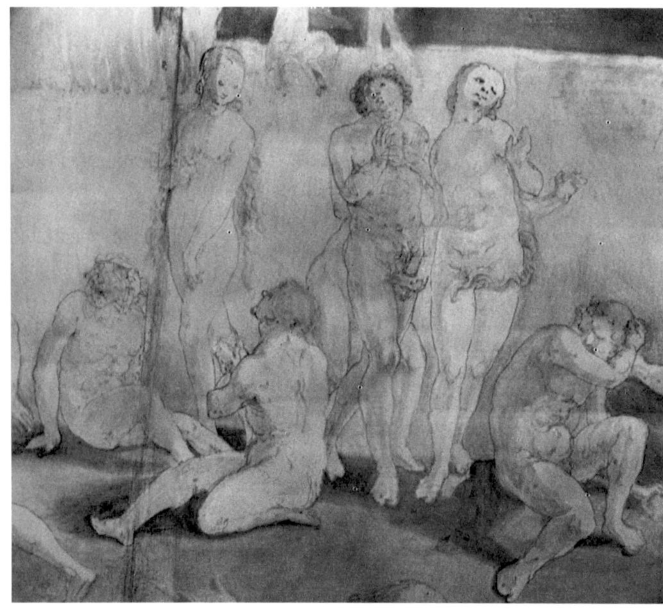

EXAMINING PAINTINGS WITH X-RAY PHOTOGRAPHY

A whole range of methods have been developed in the past century for examining the structure of paint layers and identifying pigments and media, but they will not be discussed here. Another important method for getting a better idea of the structure of the paint layers and the support (panel or canvas), is x-ray photography, which was first used to examine paintings in the 1920s. Pigments with a high atomic weight, such as lead white, lead-tin yellow, vermilion and azurite, absorb the x-rays and show up white in the x-radiograph. It also reveals additions to a panel: nails, dowels, strips of wood

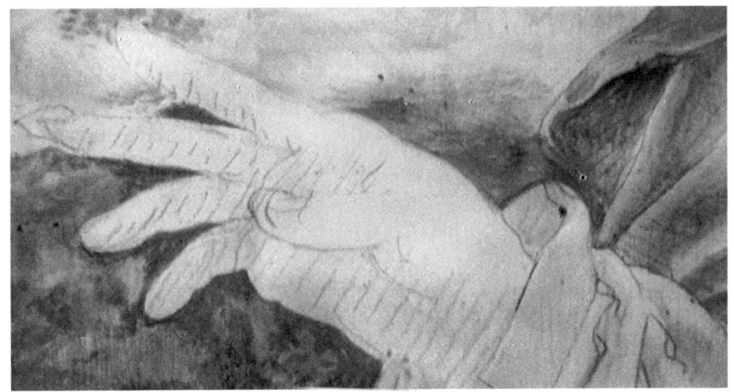

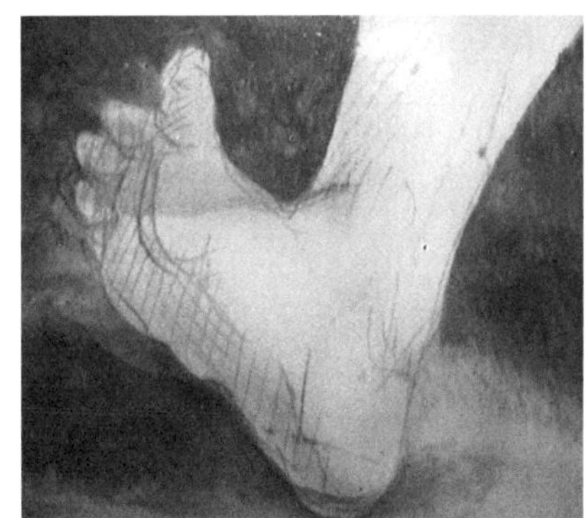

37 a-b
IRR assemblies of the outer wings of the *Triptych with the Last Judgement* (fig. 25), with an underdrawing in black chalk of Paul's hand and foot. The saints were indicated sketchily with black chalk, with a few contours and straight hatchings, but the underdrawing was not always followed faithfully in the paint. Paul's foot, for instance, pointed upwards far more in the underdrawing and the reserve.

and cradling, as well as changes made during the painting process and later additions, and sometimes the way in which a scene was painted. The x-radiographs of *The dance around the golden calf* published here provide information about the structure of the panel and the paint layers (figs. 33, 39), and reveal the draughtsman-like way in which the artist applied the paint in the faces, and the structure of the clothing and other passages (fig. 39).

THE UNDERDRAWING

The underdrawing in the relatively small group of undoubted paintings by Lucas van Leyden were investigated with infrared reflectography a few decades ago, and that yielded some fascinating results.

It was hardly surprising to discover that Lucas was a virtuoso draughtsman who prepared his early figure paintings (figs. 16, 18) extremely carefully with a delicate brush drawing on the layer of ground. The faces and the shaded areas in the clothing were painstakingly drawn with elegant lines (fig. 34). The inner wings of the *Triptych with the Last Judgement* (fig. 26) also have a meticulous, washed drawing done with a brush (figs. 35, 36), while the outer wings have a fairly sketchy chalk underdrawing (fig. 37). The washed brush drawing, in which the wash was used to model the flesh passages, is unique in early Netherlandish painting, as far as is known. Changes were made in many of the figures and poses during the painting process, and these were indicated with chalk (fig. 36). On the outer wings with Sts Peter and Paul it can be seen that alterations were made to the hands and feet relative to the chalk drawing and the reserves (fig. 37).

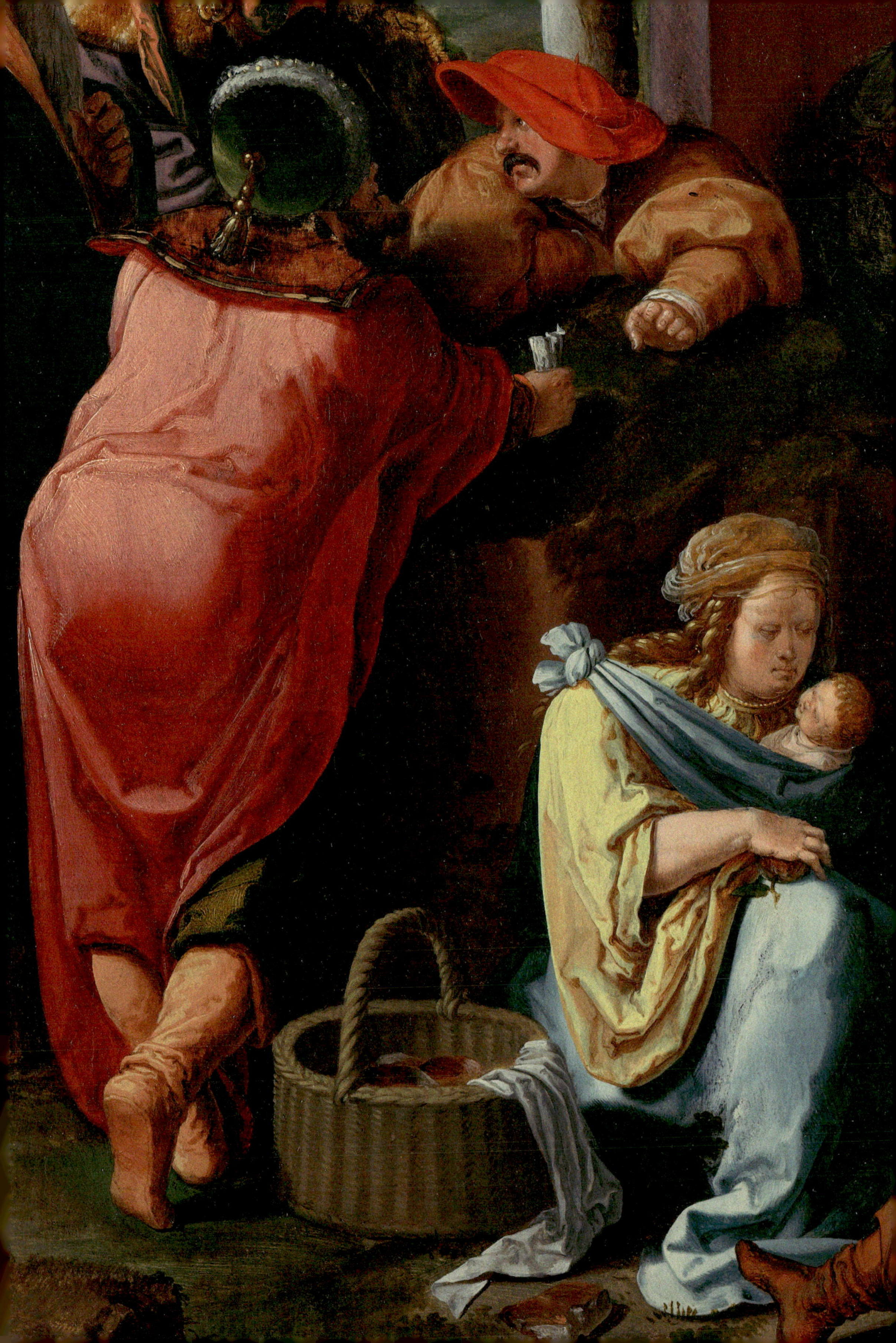

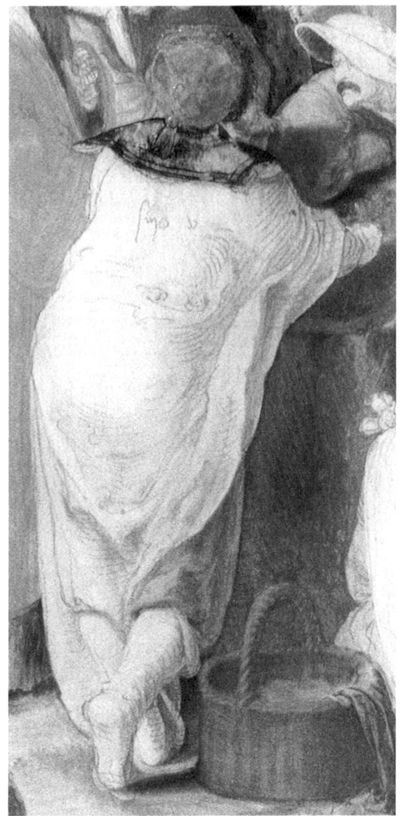

38 >
IRR assembly of the standing man seen from the back on the left panel of *The dance around the golden calf*, in which the green and brown passages are impenetrable. The chalk underdrawing has parallel hatchings, which follow the shape of the cloak, to indicate where the shadows were to be placed. The notations 'sino' and 'v' on the man's back denote the colours to be used for painting his robe: a combination of red ('sino' for vermilion) and white ('v').

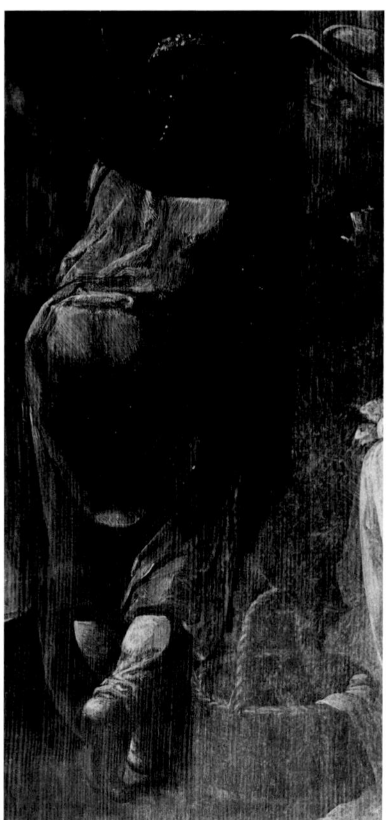

39 >>
x-ray photograph of the same detail shows how the light passages in the cloak were drawn with very fine strokes in the white paint and the pink underpaint. The shaded passages painted with a red glaze show up as black. The efficient and draughtsman-like way in which the fairly dry paint was applied is clearly seen in the x-ray.

< 40
Detail from the left wing: the man seen from the back and the seated woman with a baby.

THE UNDERDRAWING IN *THE DANCE AROUND THE GOLDEN CALF*

The underdrawing on the triptych was done with black chalk in a rapid and rather cursory fashion, with little attention to the details. The parts of it that are illustrated here show that it and the paint were applied in a similar way on the centre panel as well as the wings. The foreground figures were prepared quite carefully with contours in the faces and bodies, and hatching and cross-hatching in the shaded areas. The figures in the middleground are much sketchier, being indicated with only a few lines and little hatching. The drawing was used to make the reserves for the figures in the background and the landscape, which appears in the infrared reflectograms as a dark area with hardly any underdrawing.

One gets a good idea of the artist's working method by comparing an infrared reflectogram assembly of the underdrawing (fig. 38) and an x-radiograph (fig. 39) with a detail photograph of the same area on the painted surface (fig. 40). The folds in the garments of the man seen from the back on the left wing are indicated with some scrawly lines and a few curly ones, with curved parallel hatchings for the shaded areas (fig. 38). The underdrawing had an important function when it came to applying the light and shaded areas of the clothing. This is revealed by the x-radiograph, which shows how carefully the modelling of the standing man's red cloak was applied with a fine brush in white paint on the red underpaint (fig. 39). Another good example is the underdrawing of the seated woman with a baby to the right of the man seen from the back (figs. 40, 41). The dark areas in her skirt are indicated with cross-hatchings, with straight parallel hatching being used for the shadow on her face (fig. 41). Her blue skirt is almost white in the area that catches the light, and is dark blue in the shadowed area. This colour transition is indicated in the underdrawing with colour notations: 'v' for white and 'b' for blue (fig. 43).

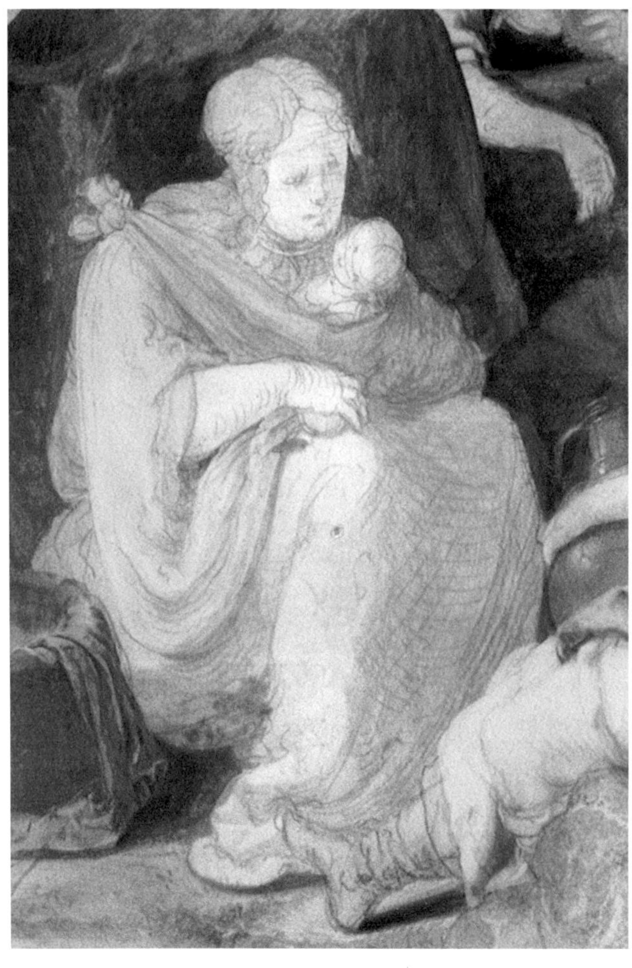

41
IRR assembly of the underdrawing of the seated woman with a baby on the left wing. Her face was turned to her left in the underdrawing, and parallel hatchings on the right side of her face indicate the shadow. The baby's tiny head is very cursorily drawn. Cross-hatchings in the woman's blue robe show where the dark blue shaded passages were to be painted. The letters 'v' and 'b' in the light part of the robe denote the colour combination to be used there: white and blue.

COLOUR NOTATIONS IN THE UNDERDRAWING

This brings us to the function of the colour notations, of which there are 30 at 20 different points in the underdrawing. Notations of this kind are found on early Netherlandish and German paintings, but rarely in such numbers. Some of those on *The dance around the golden calf* are fairly easy to read and interpret, such as the 'b' for blue, 'v' for white (sometimes combined with 'p' for 'plumber', or lead white) and 'm' for massicot (yellow). Most of the notations relate to red, which is indicated in three different ways, with 'ro' ('rood'), 'sino' for sinoper (vermilion) and 'so' ('solfer'). 'Gron' is green. Two notations are used in some cases to mark the transition between colours, such as 'v' for white with 'b' (blue) (fig. 41), or with 'so' (red) (fig. 42). These colour notations were probably used as a guide for the underpainting. In view of the refined execution of the paint layer as a whole, and the small size of the triptych, it is hard to imagine that Lucas van Leyden would have left the underpainting to a workshop assistant. The colour notations must therefore have been a guide for the artist himself.

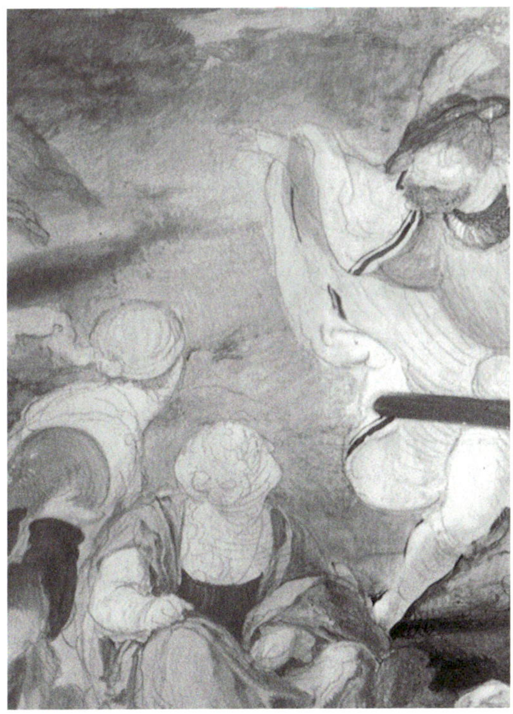

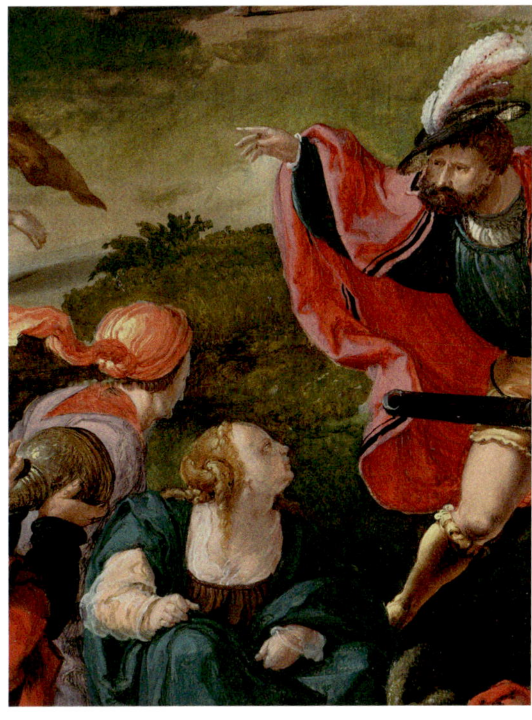

42
IRR assembly of the underdrawing on the right of the centre panel. The face of the woman looking upwards is indicated with just a few lines. On the right, in the man's red cloak, is a colour notation, the first two letters of which are an abbreviation for red.

THE STRUCTURE OF THE PAINT LAYERS

Generally speaking, the paint seems to have been applied in two layers. The light and dark passages are modelled on the underpaint, and occasionally light, transparent highlights were added on top, or shaded areas were reinforced with a little black paint (fig. 46). From the very outset, most of the light passages were built up differently from the dark ones of the same colour. The light areas in the red garments usually have a whitish or pink underpaint with a thin red glaze (a transparent red) on top. In the dark areas there is merely a red glaze, which is thickest in the darkest areas (fig. 40). In blue passages, the light areas are light blue and the shadows dark blue (fig. 44), and sometimes a red-brown underpaint seems to have been used for even darker passages. Ochre was used for the shaded areas in the yellows, and lead-tin yellow for the light ones. The combination of the underdrawing, hatchings and colour notations were a precise basis for applying the paint layers in light and darker areas, which contrast quite strongly.
The figures at the transition to the middleground were drawn a little more cursorily, but nevertheless with a remarkable feel for characteristic details (figs. 42, 46), which were worked up in the very colourful surface. The facial features were drawn in the wet paint with a fine brush, with light highlights, brown lines and occasional scratches in the paint (fig. 46).

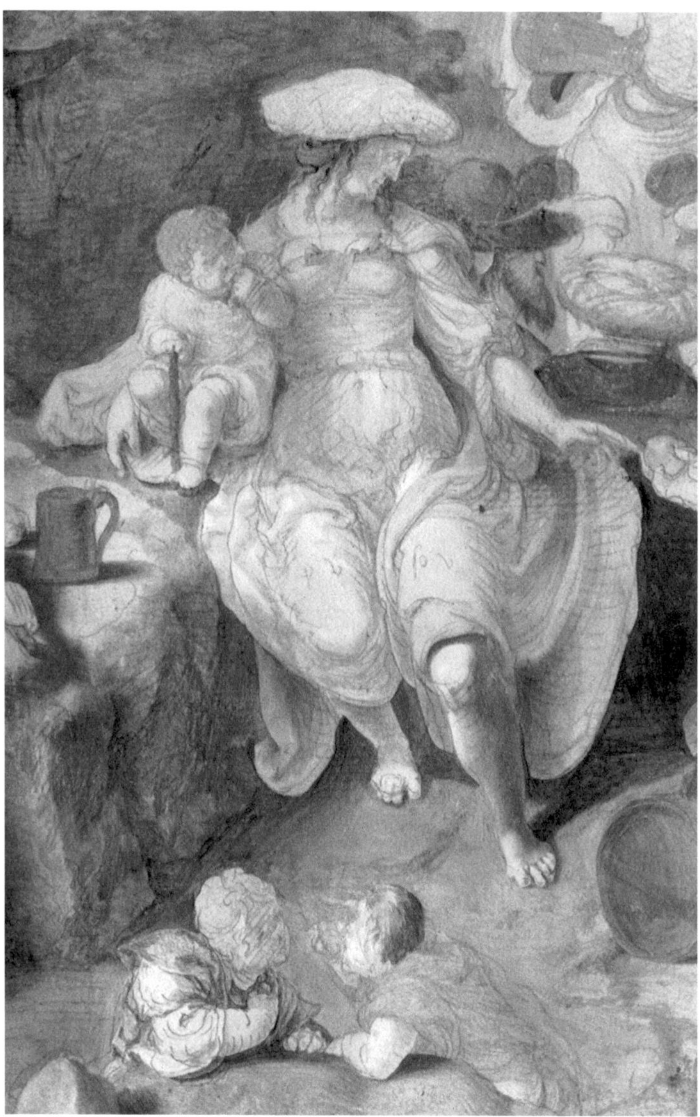

43
IRR assembly of the under-drawing beneath the seated woman with a child in the centre panel. Her robe is indicated with a great variety of lines, straight, parallel and cross-hatchings to mark out the shaded areas in the blue and red robes. On her right knee she has the letters 'p' and 'v', short for lead white, denoting the light part of her blue robe. To the right, in the red cloak on her left knee, are the letters 'so' (red), 'v' (white) and 'b' (blue).

44 >
Detail of the seated woman with a child on the centre panel.

The small groups of figures in the middleground dancing around the golden calf and beneath the trees on the right were far more sketchily prepared with a few lines and hatchings that give the figures some volume (fig. 45). Most of the heads are merely indicated with ovals. The distinctive movements of the dancing figures, though, were captured brilliantly. The figures themselves were painted sketchily with light pastel tints. A great deal of care was taken over the landscape with green trees in the background. The atmo-

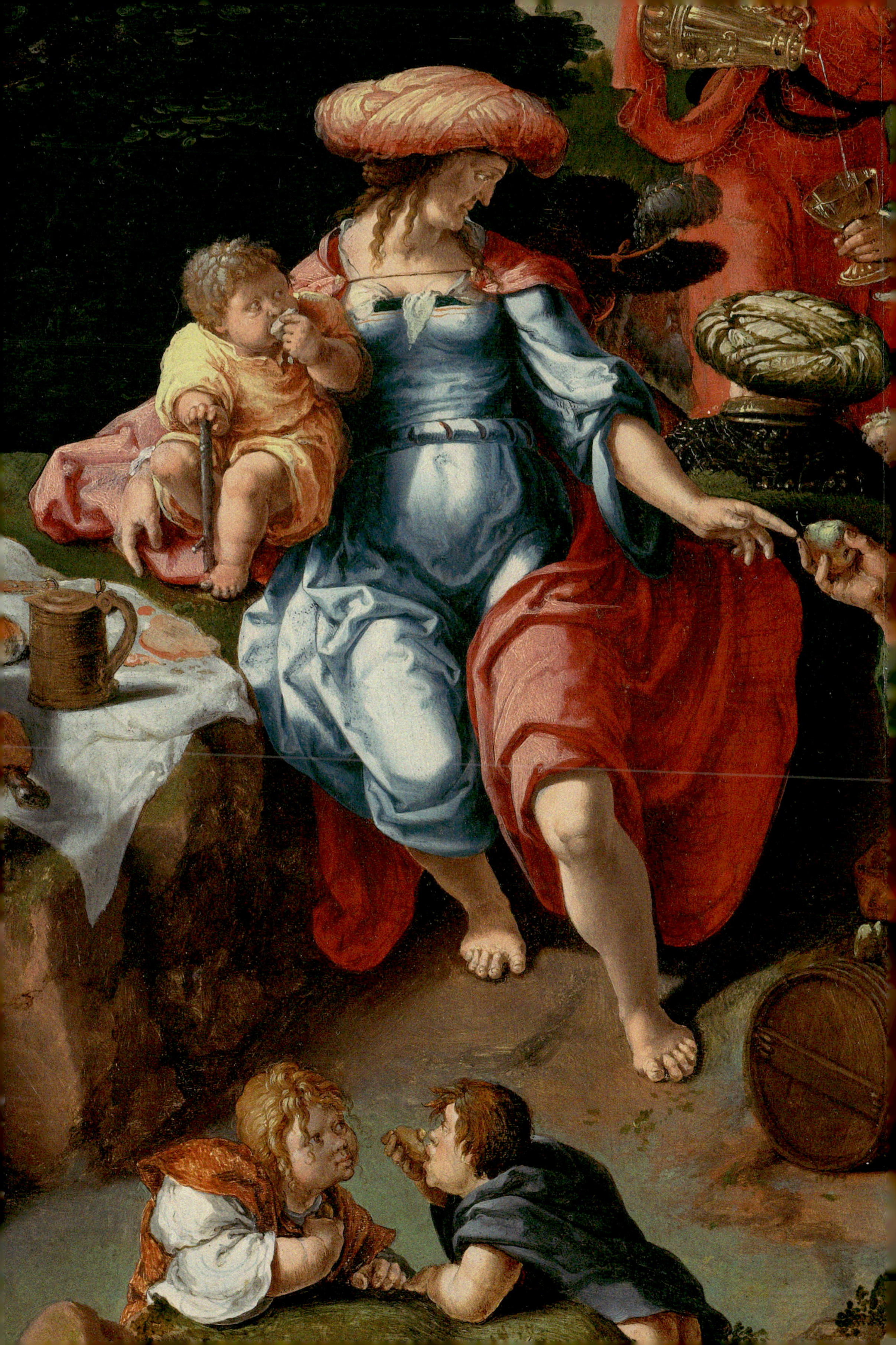

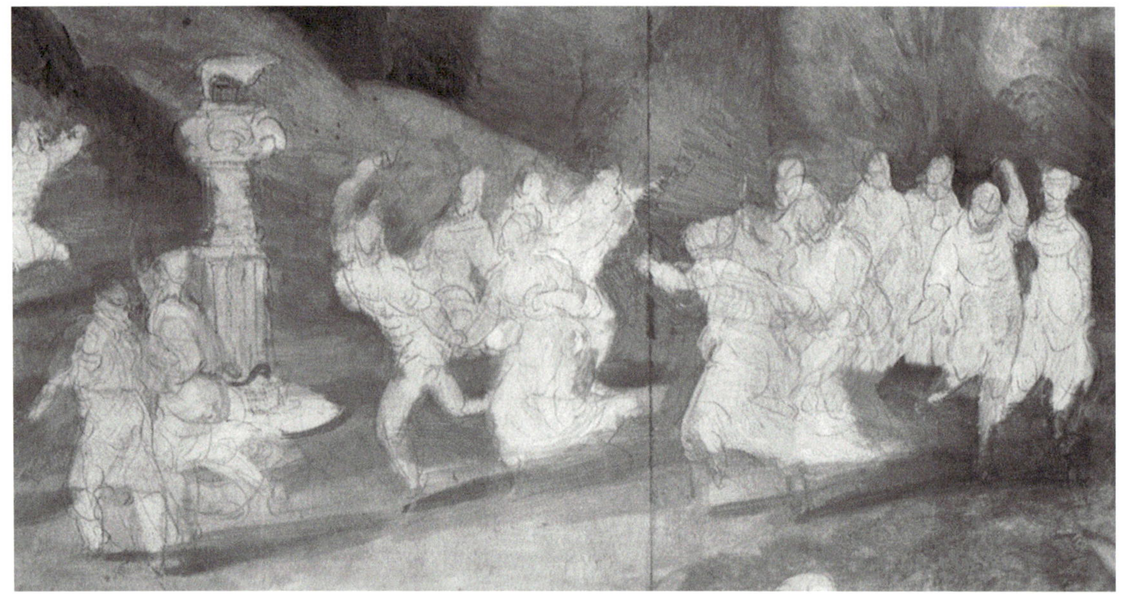

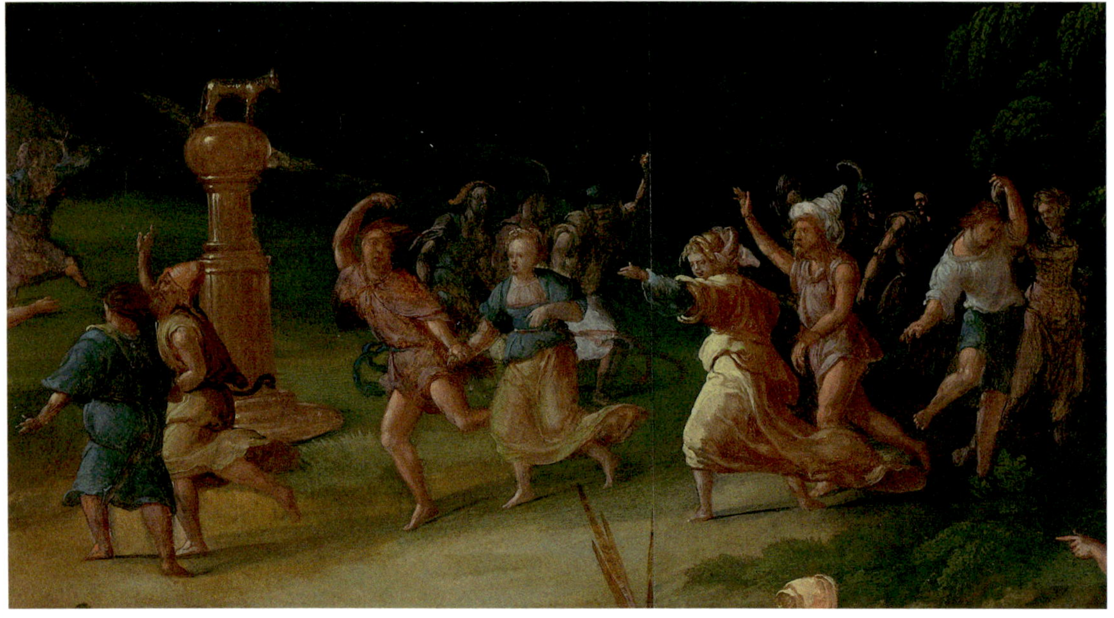

45 a-b
Detail of the group of dancing figures to the right of the golden calf and the IRR assembly of the underdrawing of the same detail. The figures were reserved in the background on the basis of the extremely cursory underdrawing, and painted sketchily in light colours.

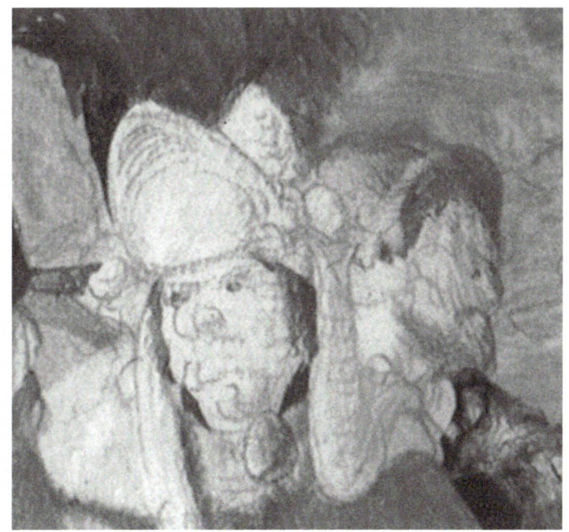

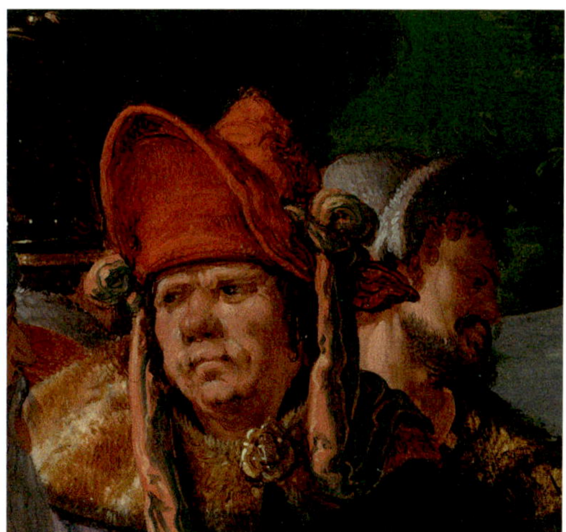

46a-b
Detail of the man with a bulbous nose and a red mitre and the IRR assembly of the underdrawing of the same detail. The face and the mitre were modelled in a very lively way in the wet paint on the basis of the cursory underdrawing.

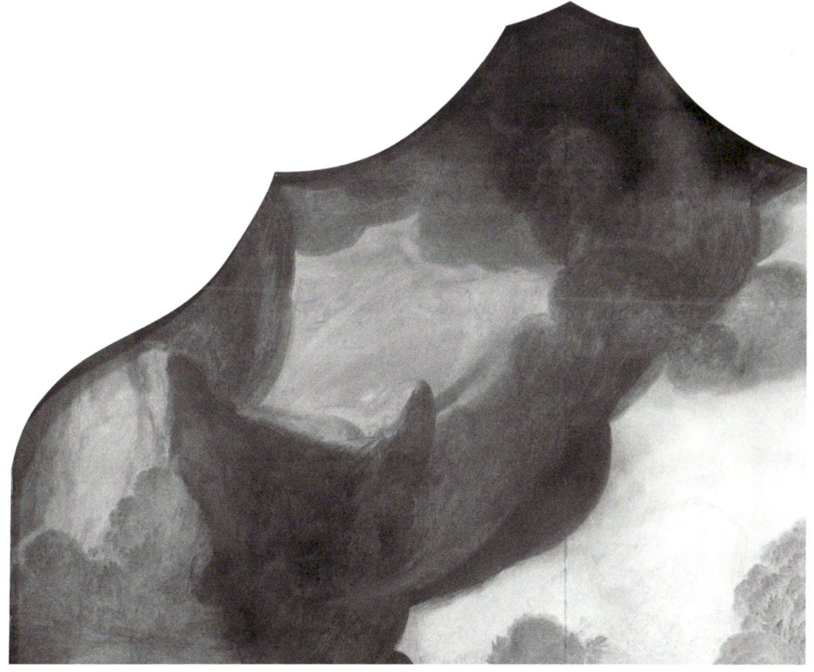

47
Infrared reflectography reveals the dark underpainting of the clouds in which God the Father appeared to Moses. The latter was reserved as a minuscule figure on the projecting finger of rock. The light area of cloud was initially planned to be smaller.

pheric recession to the blue sky was well executed with greenish and then blue mountains.

No underdrawing could be detected in this area with infrared reflectography. It does, though, reveal the dark underpaint of the clouds in which God appears to Moses. Above him there are massive dark clouds, but apart from that there is no indication of God's presence (fig. 47).

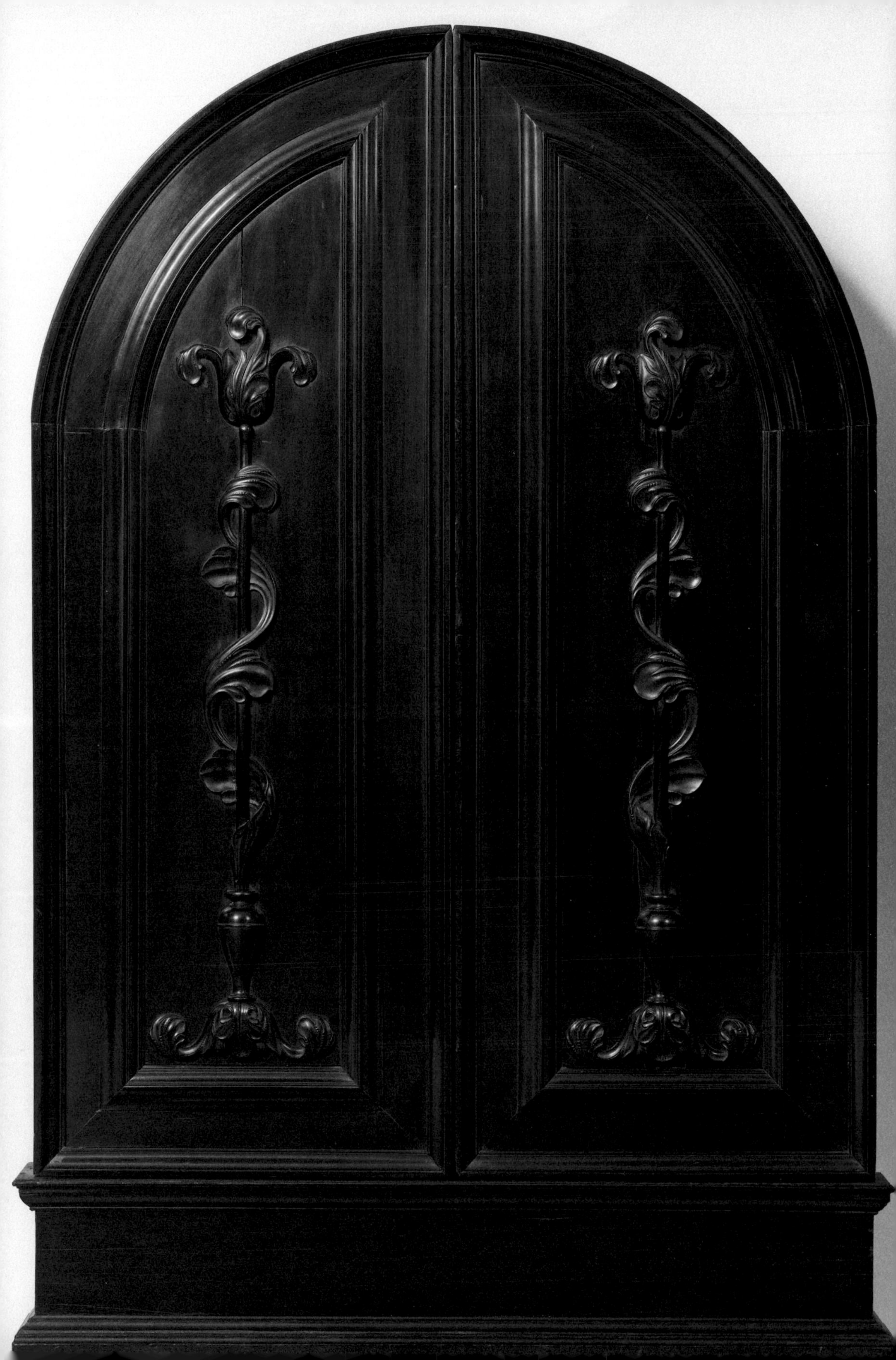

The former owners of *The dance*

Nothing is known about the person who commissioned and first owned *The dance around the golden calf*. As already mentioned, Van Mander says that the 'cabinet' was in Kalverstraat in Amsterdam when he wrote his *Schilder-boeck* in 1604. The Amsterdam archive researcher Sebastiaan Dudok van Heel put forward the plausible theory that it belonged to a descendant of the Van Swieten family of Leiden, who had commissioned the *Triptych with the Last Judgement*, and interestingly there was an Aegje van Swieten who lived at 45 Kalverstraat. Evidence that Karel van Mander had seen the triptych is provided by his own painting of the subject of 1602, in which he borrowed elements from Lucas van Leyden's composition (fig. 49).

48
The doors of the seventeenth-century ebony frame (see p. 55), the 'beautiful cabinet'. Closed, showing the tulip motif on each door.

49
Karel van Mander, *The dance around the golden calf*, 1602. Oil on canvas, 98 x 213.5 cm. Frans Hals Museum, Haarlem. The structure of Van Mander's painting shows that he knew Lucas van Leyden's version in Amsterdam. The scene of the actual dance is based on the one in the triptych.

THE DANCE AROUND THE GOLDEN CALF WITH SEVENTEENTH-CENTURY COLLECTORS

It is known that the triptych was owned by the Amsterdam banker Jaspar Losschaert (Loskaert) (?-1658) in the 1650s. The first evidence of this provenance is an annotation in a copy of Van Mander's *Schilder-boeck* belonging to Hendrik Houmes, a lawyer of Medemblik, who in 1671 wrote in the margin beside the passage about *The dance*: 'I saw this piece in Amsterdam, on Herengracht, with Mr Wuytiers, who had been bequeathed it by Jaspar Losschaert'. This provenance has since been confirmed by Dudok van Heel. The bachelor Jaspar Losschaert lived at 214 Herengracht with the family of his nephew Dirck Wuytiers. His collection also contained the famous *Darmstadt Madonna* by Hans Holbein the

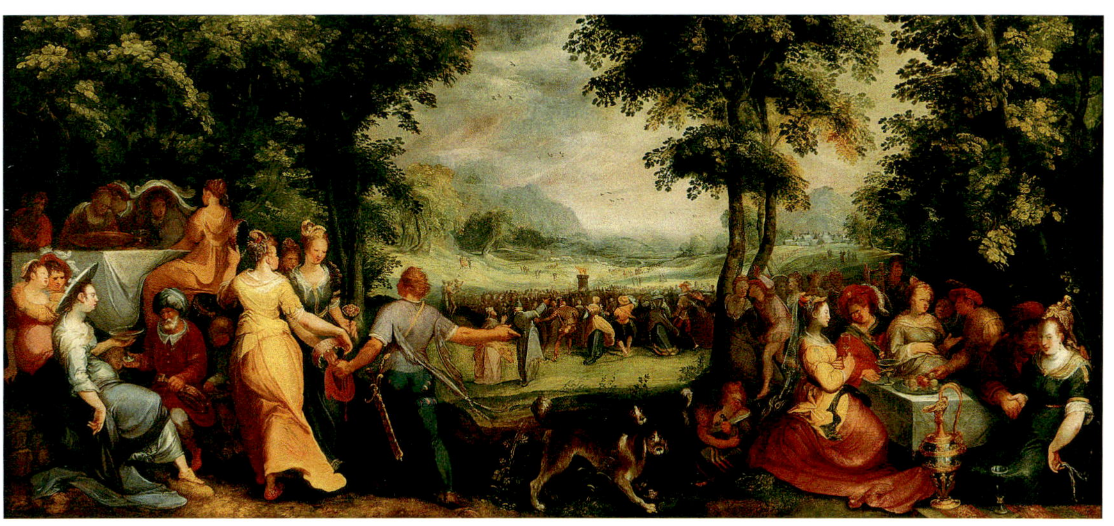

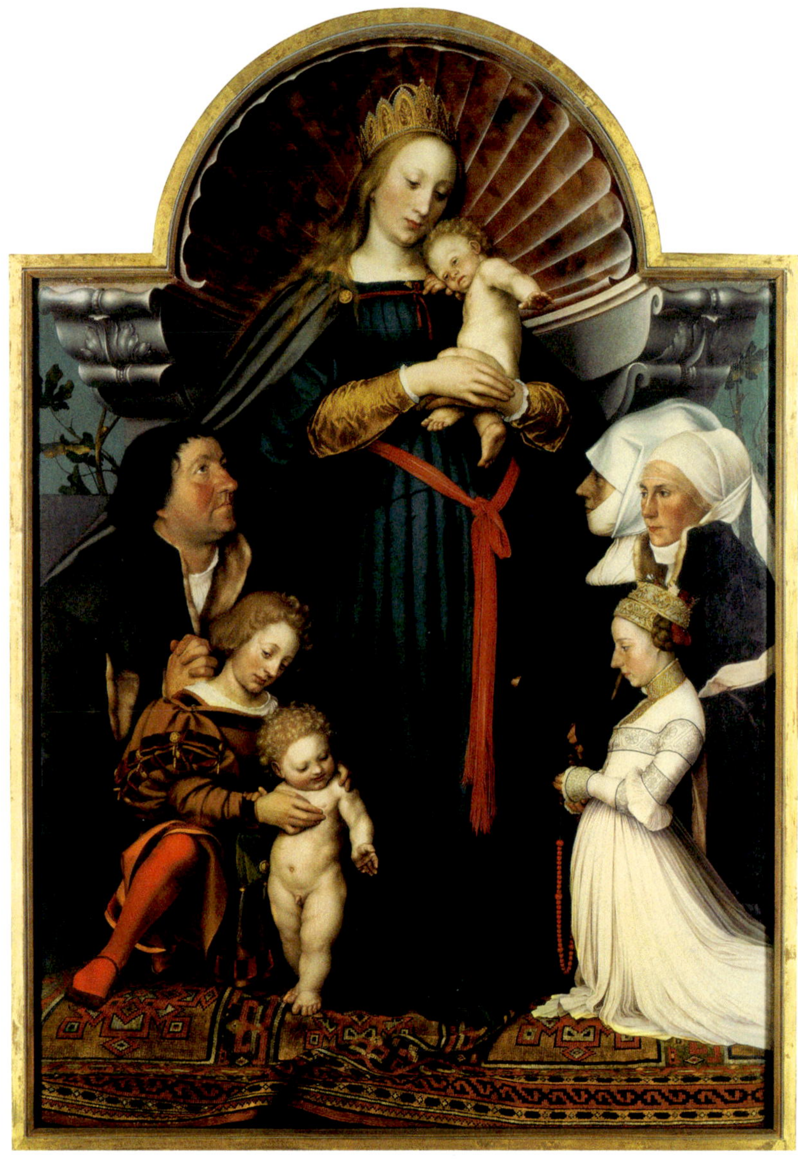

50
Hans Holbein the Younger, *The Meyer family with the Virgin, the Christ Child and the infant John the Baptist, also known as The Darmstadt Madonna*, c. 1525-29. Oil on panel, 146.5 x 102 cm. Städelsches Kunstinstitut, Frankfurt, on loan from the Hessische Hausstiftung. This famous painting remained in Basel until 1638, when it was bought through the Amsterdam art dealer Michel le Blon by Jaspar Losschaert, who also owned Lucas van Leyden's triptych and other important sixteenth-century paintings (figs. 51, 52). Le Blon had a copy of it made by Bartholomeus Sarburgh for other potential customers. In the nineteenth century that copy, by then in Dresden, was long regarded as the original. The latter and other paintings from Losschaert came into the possession of Jacob Cromhout, whose collection was auctioned after his death in 1709. In the nineteenth century it was owned by the grand dukes of Hesse in Darmstadt.

Younger (fig. 50), which he had bought from the Amsterdam art dealer Michel le Blon around 1638. On his death in 1658, Losschaert left his collection to his second cousin Jacob Wuytiers (c. 1613-79), who continued living in his parents' house on Herengracht and never married. In addition to *The dance* and the Holbein, the collection contained a *Madonna* and a *Hercules and Deianeira* by Jan Gossaert (fig. 51), *The fall of man* by Frans Floris, and *Christ in the house of Martha and Mary* by Pieter Aertsen (fig. 52). The collector, who also owned drawings by Albrecht Dürer, had an interest in northern art of the sixteenth century that was rare for his time.

The six paintings are listed in Jacob Wuytiers's will of 1679, in which he

left his collection of 51 paintings, drawings (by Dürer, among others) and his library to his eldest nephew, Dirck Wuytiers. The latter gave the collection of paintings to his brother-in-law, Jacob Cromhout (1651-1708), who was married to his sister Margaretha Wuytiers. Cromhout moved the paintings to his house at 364 Herengracht, one of the four Cromhout houses built for his father by the famous architect Philips Vingboons in 1660-62.
In the large collection of paintings belonging to the Catholic merchant Jacob Cromhout, the mostly sixteenth-century paintings inherited from Losschaert and Wuytiers were given a place alongside important Flemish and Dutch seventeenth-century works, many of religious subjects, by artists

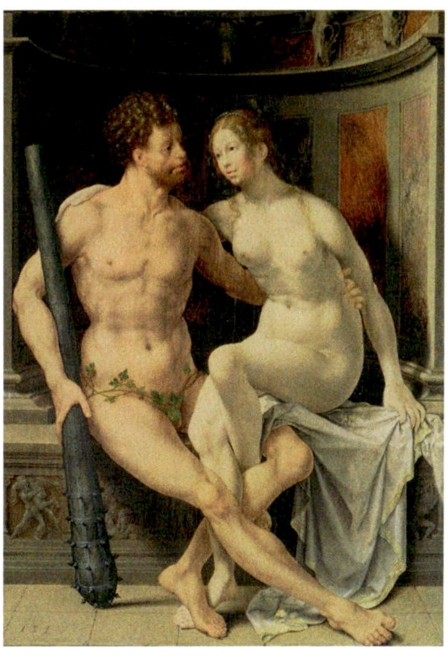

51
Jan Gossaert, *Hercules and Deianeira*, 1517. Oil on panel, 36.5 x 26 cm. The Barber Institute of Fine Arts, University of Birmingham. In addition to an *Adam and Eve* by Frans Floris, Losschaert owned this or a similar painting ('a small painting') with nude figures by Gossaert, which demonstrates his interest in Netherlandish Renaissance art.

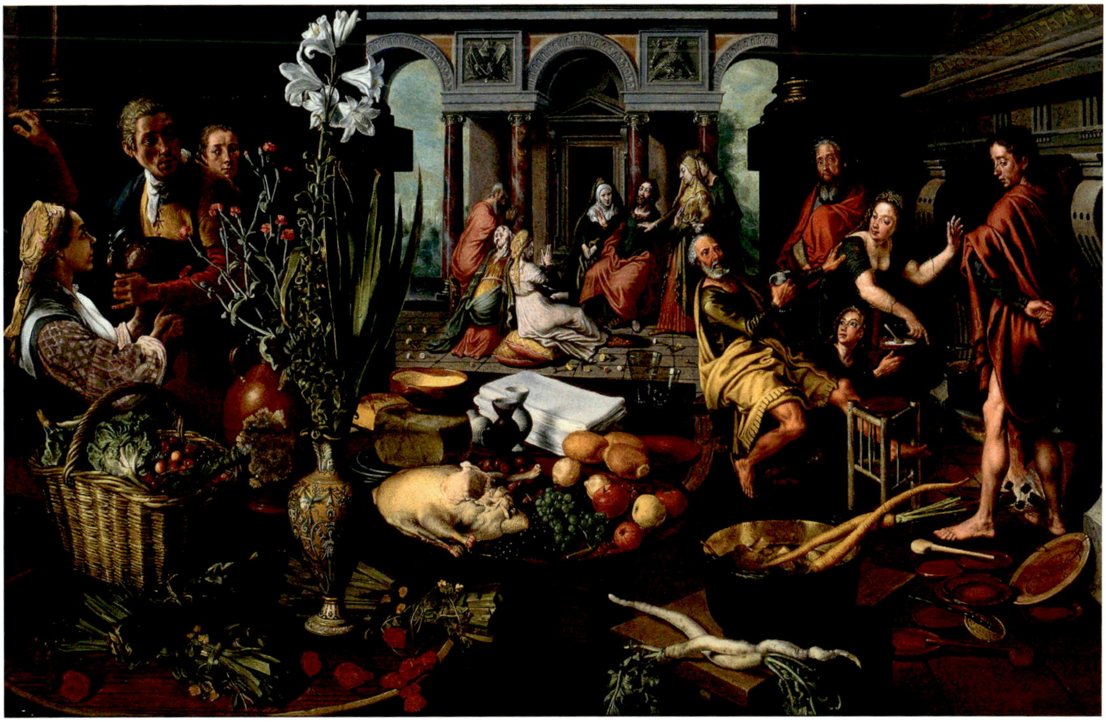

52
Pieter Aertsen, *Christ in the house of Martha and Mary*, 1553. Oil on panel, 126 x 200 cm. Museum Boijmans Van Beuningen, Rotterdam. It is likely that this or a similar large painting came from Losschaert's collection.

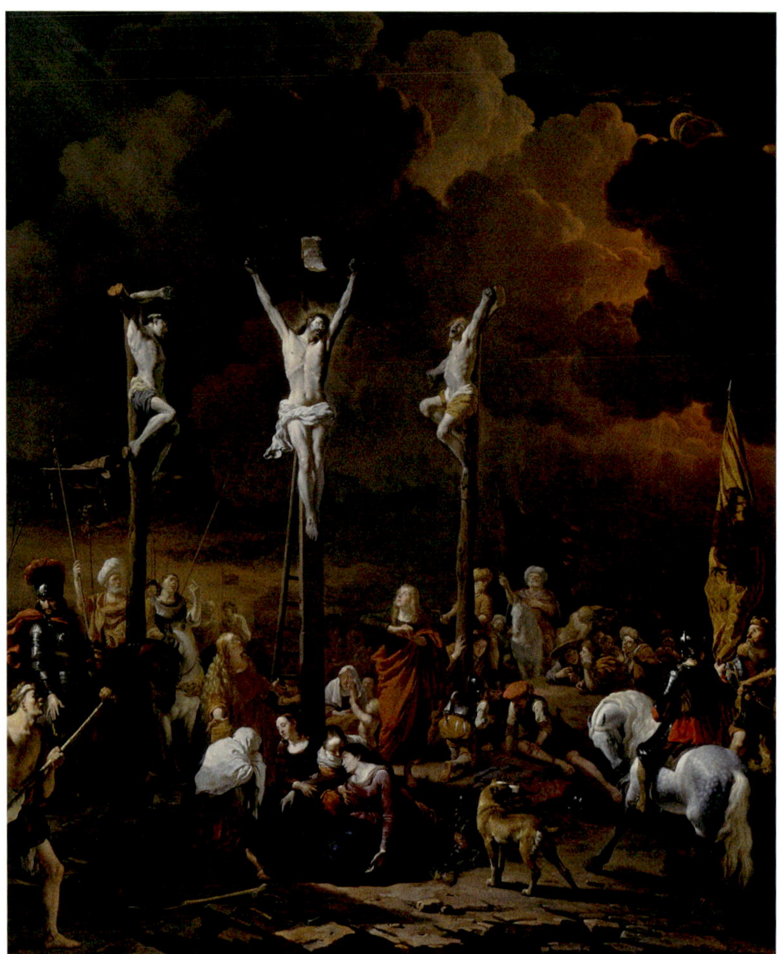

53
Karel du Jardin, *The Crucifixion*, 1661. Oil on panel, 97 x 84 cm. Musée du Louvre, Paris. The famous poet Jan Vos published a eulogy of this painting as early as 1662. Jacob Cromhout bought it at auction in 1697 for 1,330 guilders. It was sold for 1,900 guilders at the sale of his collection in 1709, a little less than the Holbein.

such as Rubens, Jacob Jordaens, Karel du Jardin, Jan Steen and Philips Wouwerman.

The 200 paintings in Jacob Cromhout's collection were auctioned on 7 and 8 May 1709 in the house where he had died, 'on Herengracht, near Huidenstraat'. The title page of the catalogue states that the sale included 'some artistic works from the cabinet of the late Jaspar Losschaert'. Rubens's altarpiece with *The coronation of the Virgin* was sold for 1,000 guilders, while *The Crucifixion* by Karel du Jardin ('uncommonly full of figures and marvellously painted') went for no less than 1,900 guilders. These were remarkably high prices for the day. Of the paintings from the Losschaert collection, Holbein's *Madonna* fetched the most, 2,000 guilders, and 1,470 guilders were paid for Lucas's *Dance*. The sale catalogue makes express mention of the frame around the latter painting: 'Where they dance around the golden calf, with a crowd of figures, by Lucas van Leyden, in a beautiful cabinet, uncommonly fine'.

A 'BEAUTIFUL CABINET': THE EBONY FRAME

The 'beautiful cabinet' was undoubtedly a reference to the heavy, arched, ornately moulded ebony frame (fig. 54). When the wings are folded over it looks like a closed cabinet. The doors are decorated on the outside with a highly stylised tulip motif (fig. 48). There are similar motifs on the inside frame above the painted scenes. The delicate moulding running around the panels is gilded. The gilt, bracket-shaped hinges are very unusual (fig. 55). The carvings are full of lively details. The leaves have veins shaped like folds, and the flowers on the inside end in 'tails' consisting of small balls. These details indicate that this fine example of Amsterdam ebony working was made around 1630-40. Holbein's *Madonna* is described in the 1709 sale catalogue as a 'capital piece with two doors'. Rather than wings, one suspects that like *The dance around the golden calf* it had doors that could be shut like a cabinet. If so, one could assume that shortly after acquiring it in 1638, Jasper Losschaert ordered frames for his two finest works from an Amsterdam cabinetmaker. Unfortunately, the frame of the Holbein 'with two doors' has not survived.

54
The opened triptych in the ebony frame after its restoration in January 2008. The frame was probably made for Jaspar Losschaert around 1630-40 by an Amsterdam cabinetmaker.

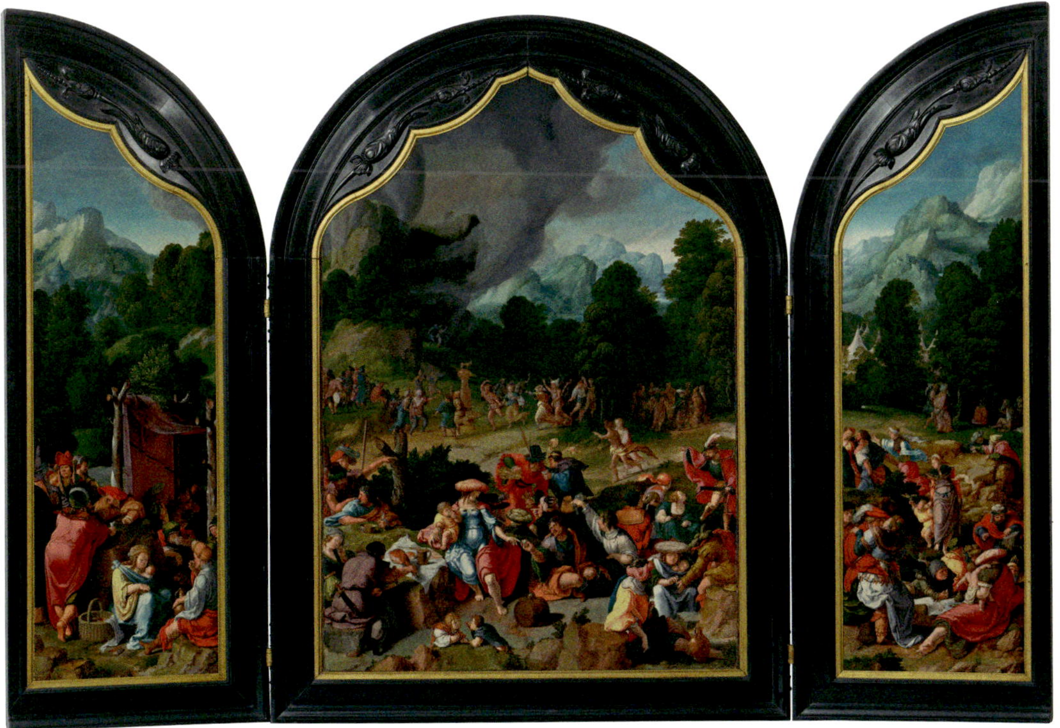

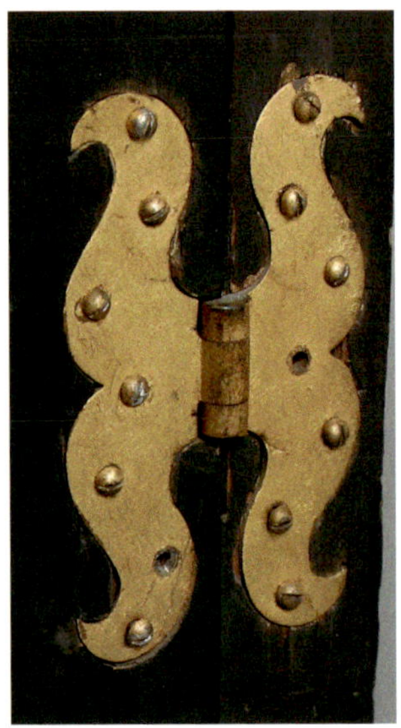

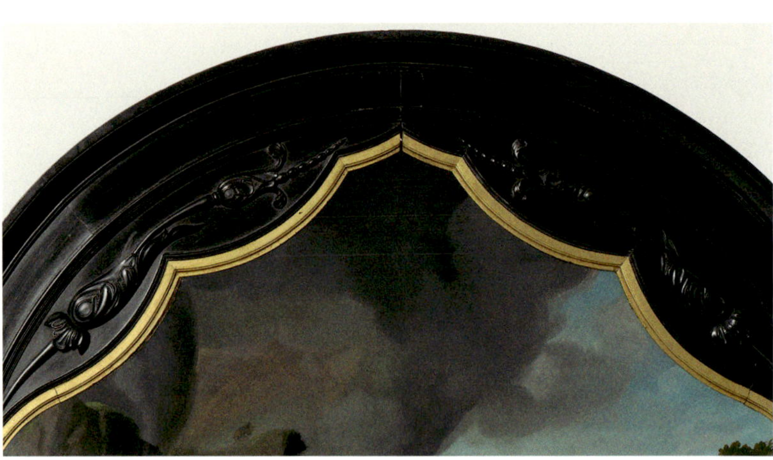

55 a-b
Details of the 'beautiful cabinet', one of the hinges, and the ornaments at the top of the frame in the middle.

56 >
Detail of the centre panel.

The ebony frame of *The dance around the golden calf* is the one that Arthur van Schendel saw when he discovered the triptych in Paris in 1952. It was then replaced with a simple, newly-made, pseudo sixteenth-century frame, complete with worm holes to make it look old. However, the old ebony frame was restored in 2007-08, and the triptych was returned to its seventeenth-century ebony setting.

LATER OWNERS OF THE DANCE

Unfortunately, it is not known who bought the triptych at the Cromhout sale. Since the Holbein came into the possession of the dukes of Lorraine, it is possible that the Lucas van Leyden entered a French collection by way of the same buyer. It only resurfaced late in the nineteenth century at the sale of the late Marquis du Blaisel's collection on 16-17 March 1870 in Paris. The cover of the catalogue hails it as a 'superb triptych by Lucas van Leyden', and the catalogue entry ends with the words: 'Nothing is lacking in this impeccable work, beautiful types of figure, correct drawing, brilliant and harmonious colouring, in the most perfect state of preservation'. It was sold for 6,200 francs to someone called Sichel. It then vanished from sight again until Van Schendel found it in the estate of Madame Bignier in Paris, when it was acquired by the Rijksmuseum.

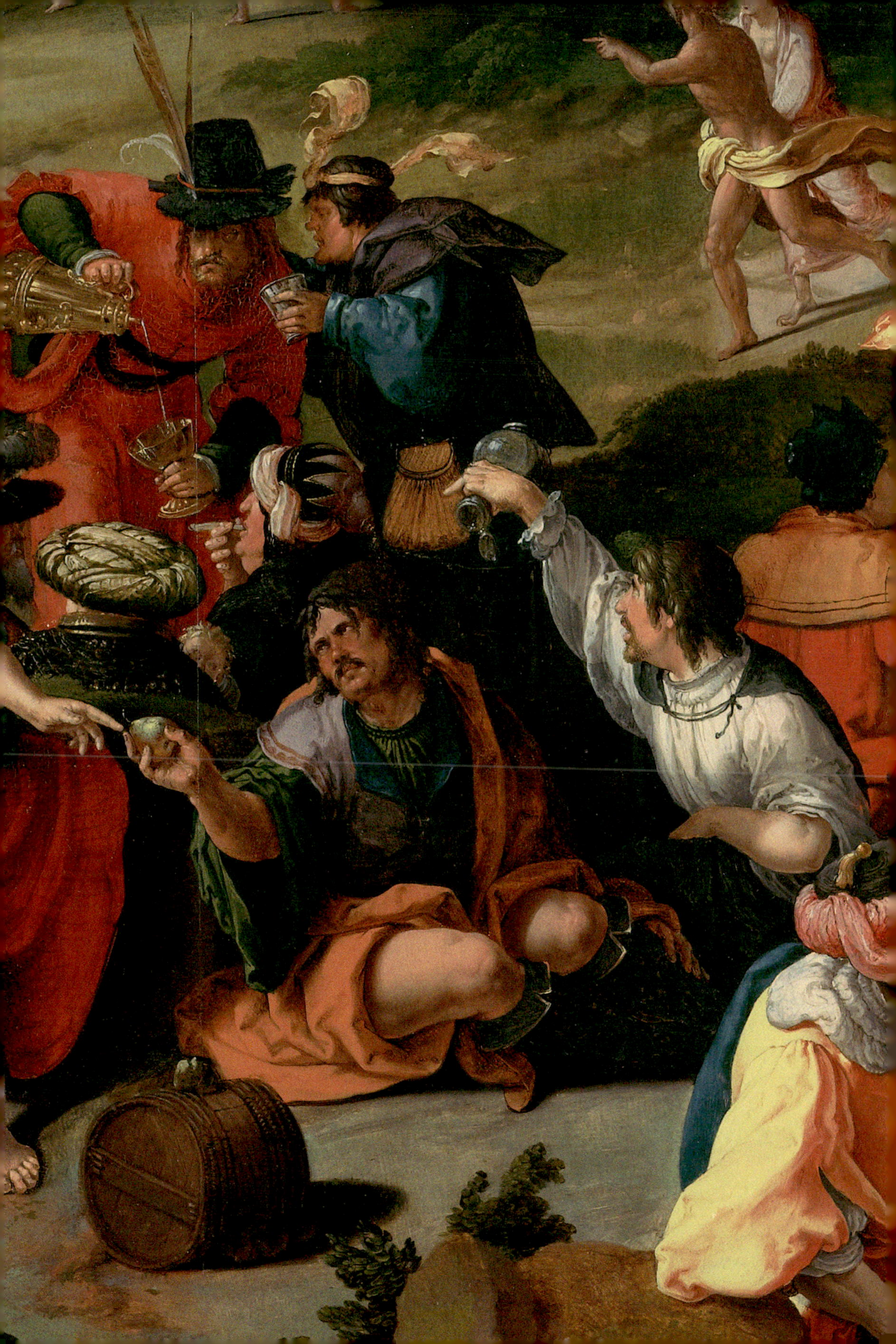

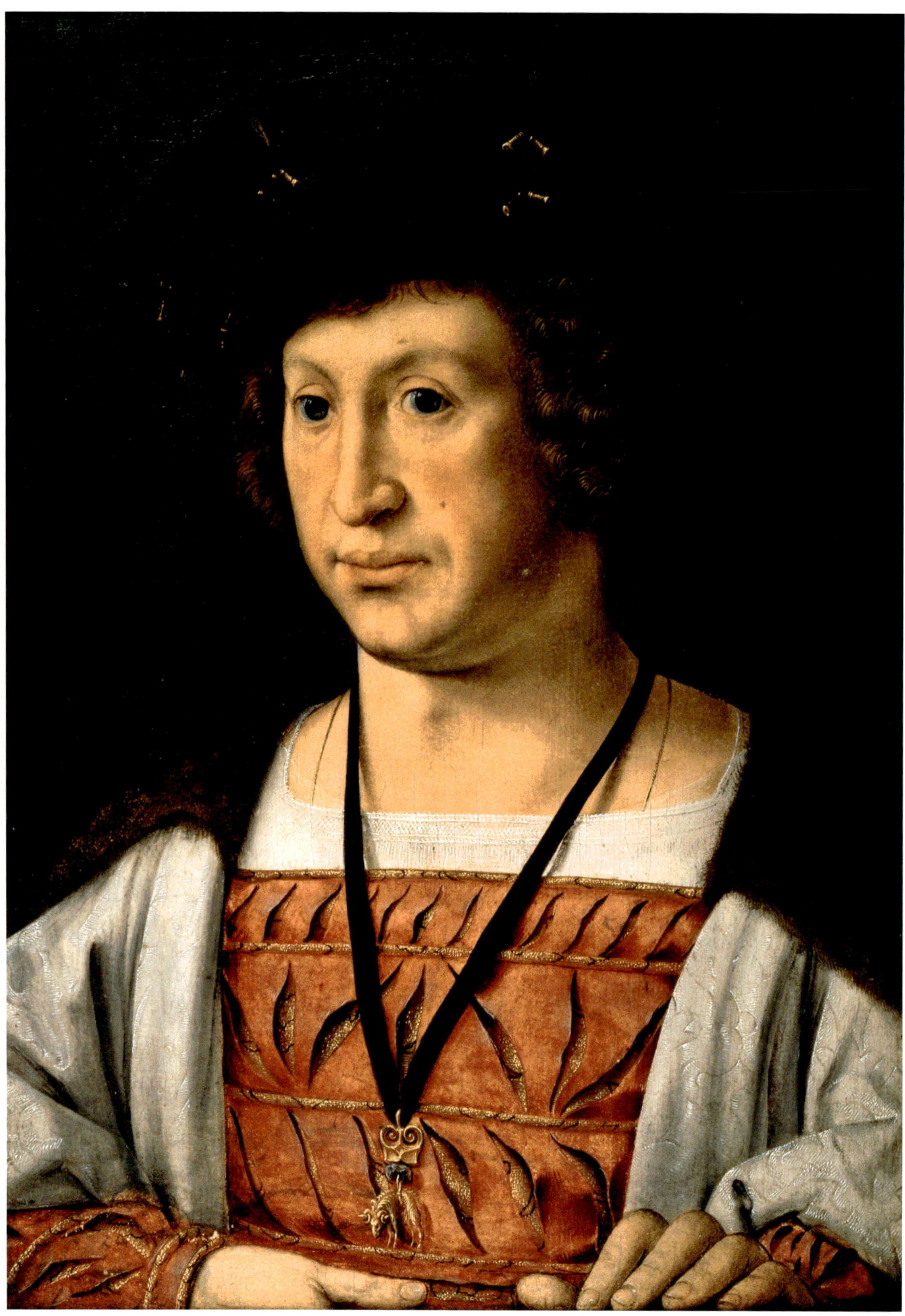

57
Jan Gossaert, *Portrait of Floris van Egmond (1469-1539), Count of Buren and Leerdam*, 1519. Oil on panel, 39.8 x 29.3 cm. Rijksmuseum, Amsterdam, on loan to the Mauritshuis, The Hague, since 1949. This portrait, which came from the stadholders' collection, was attributed to Lucas van Leyden between 1800 and 1887, and was thought to be a portrait of Philip of Burgundy. In 1887 the art historian Abraham Bredius recognised it as a work by Jan Gossaert, a contemporary of Lucas van Leyden's, and the sitter was later identified as Floris van Egmond on the basis of another portrait. It is one of the finest sixteenth-century portraits in the Rijksmuseum's collection.

The Rijksmuseum in search of the real Lucas van Leyden

Around 1800, when little was yet known about early Netherlandish art, the name of Lucas van Leyden was more of a generic label for sixteenth-century paintings, just as the name Van Eyck was for the fifteenth century. For instance, when the Koninklijk Museum opened as the national collection of paintings in the Royal Palace in Amsterdam in 1809, the catalogue listed three paintings as being by Van Eyck. We now know that one was painted by Geertgen tot Sint Jans, another gave the Master of the Virgo inter Virgines his ad hoc name, and the third is a copy after Hieronymus Bosch.

A PORTRAIT OF PHILIP OF BURGUNDY

The catalogue of 1809 also stated that a portrait of Philip of Burgundy had been painted by Lucas van Leyden (fig. 57). In 1887 it was rightly attributed to Jan Gossaert, and in the early twentieth century the sitter was identified as Floris van Egmond. The painting, which came from the collection of the stadholders and was in Honselaarsdijk Castle around 1700, is still one of the best sixteenth-century portraits in the Rijksmuseum, but is far removed from Lucas van Leyden. That attribution, though, was not entirely incomprehensible, given the early sixteenth-century dress, the style, and Lucas van Leyden's distinctive L monogram to the right of the sitter's head. It is possible that the L is not a monogram at all but the Roman number 50, indicating Floris's age when the portrait was painted.

JOANNES WTENBOGAERT'S ALBUM OF LUCAS VAN LEYDEN PRINTS

Along with the paintings in the Trippenhuis in 1817 there was the print collection of Pieter Cornelis, Baron van Leyden (1717-88), which formed the nucleus of the present-day Rijksprentenkabinet. In addition to many of the finest European prints it contains a magnificent collection of prints by Lucas van Leyden. We now know that it was actually put together in the seventeenth century by the Amsterdam collector Joannes Wtenbogaert (1608-80). As well as a few drawings (fig. 58), the album in which Wtenbogaert kept his Lucas prints contains almost the entire oeuvre of engravings, woodcuts and etchings, with the exception of a few unique impressions. All the prints by Lucan van Leyden reproduced in this book come from that album (figs. 11, 12, 14, 17, 20). This collection meant that Amsterdam had the best possible showing of the artist's prints in remarkably fine impressions. That was not the case with his paintings.

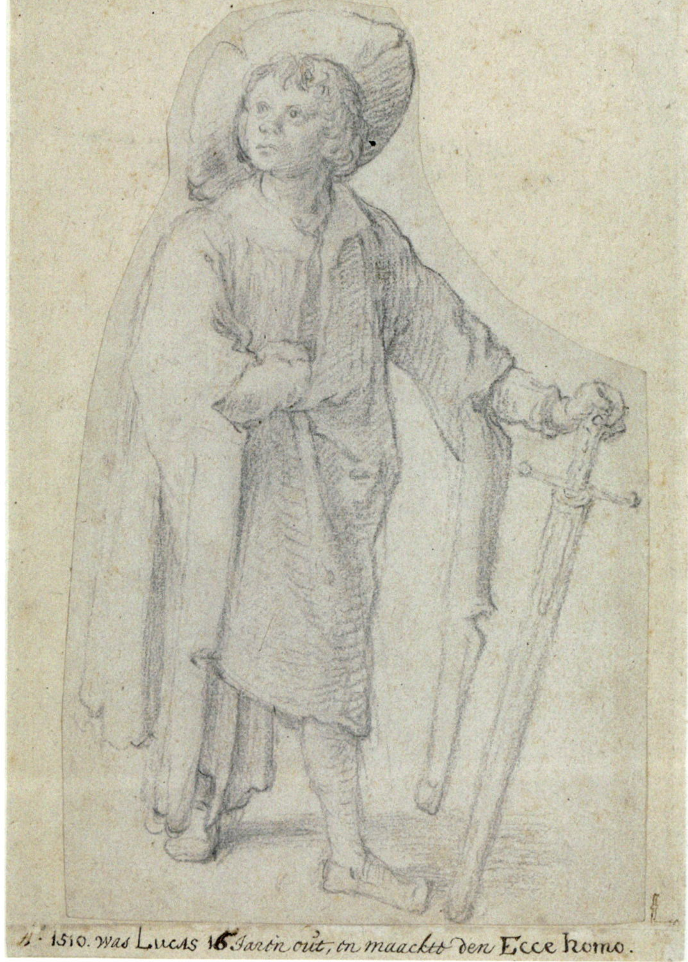

58
Lucas van Leyden, *Young man with a sword*, c. 1510. Black chalk, 24.5 x 15.8 cm. Rijksmuseum, Amsterdam. The drawing with an inscription in an old hand is from Wtenbogaert's album.

59 >
Attributed to Aertgen Claesz van Leyden, *The calling of St Antony*, c. 1530. Oil on panel, 132.6 x 96.3 cm. Rijksmuseum, Amsterdam. The purchase of this painting in 1897 was made possible by the support of the Vereniging Rembrandt. It went under the title of *The church sermon* at the time, and was seen as a work by Lucas van Leyden, being signed with the monogram L.

THE CHURCH SERMON

Victor de Stuers, the driving force behind the building of a new home for the Rijksmuseum, complained in his 1873 article 'Holland op zijn smalst' (Holland at its meanest) that 'visitors to the national museums search in vain for Lucas van Leyden, for Scorel, for Goltzius, etc.'. Until 1875, the purchase of paintings was the exception rather than the rule, but the administrators of the newly founded Rijksmuseum set out to assemble a complete overview of Dutch painting, starting from the late middle ages, despite a shortage of funds. It was not until 1897 that they succeeded in acquiring a work by Lucas van Leyden, *The church sermon*, a large painting bearing the monogram L (fig. 59). Almost half a century later doubts arose about the authenticity of the monogram and the accuracy of the attribution, but it still bore the name of Lucas van Leyden in the Rijksmuseum catalogue of 1960. That same year,

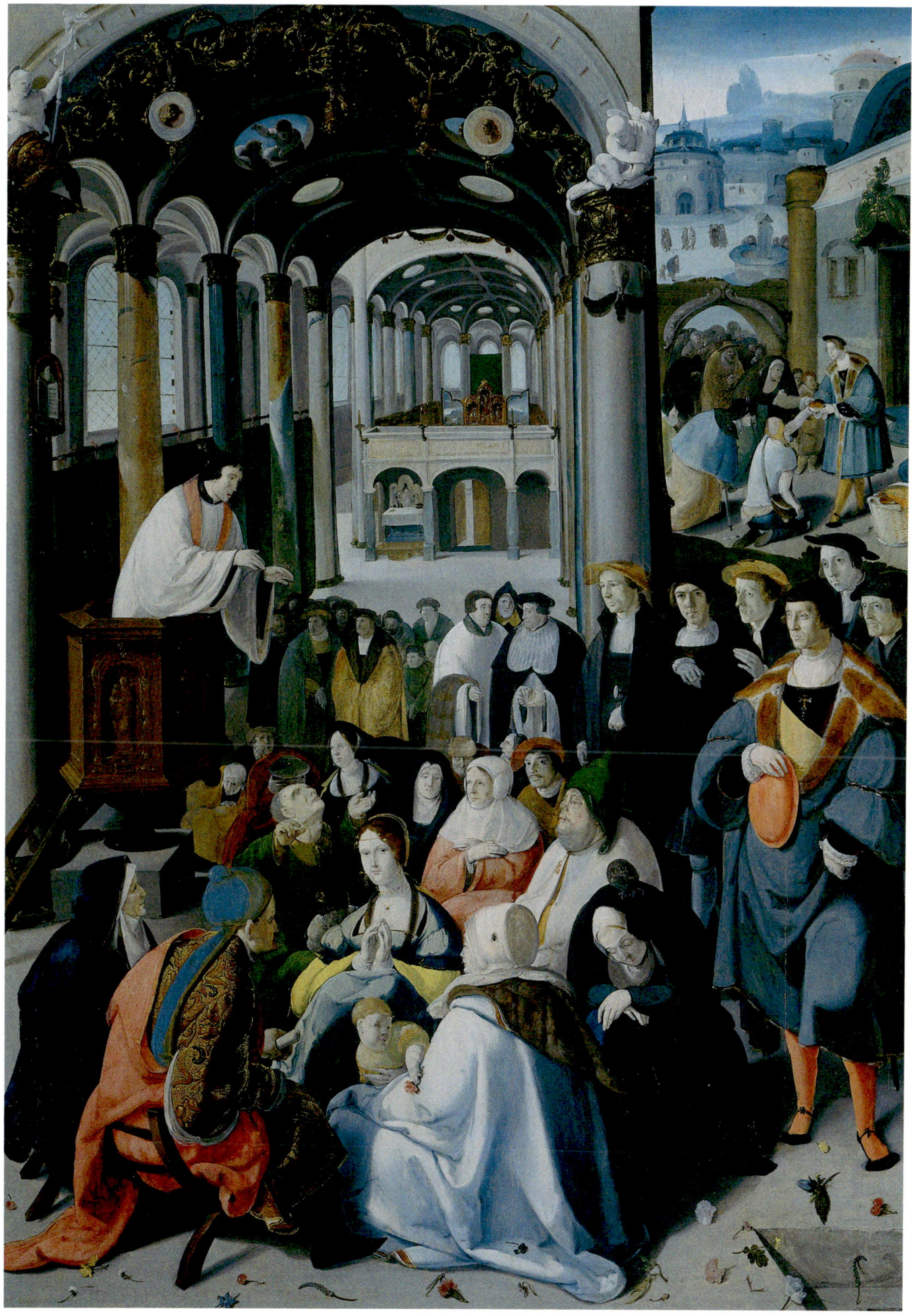

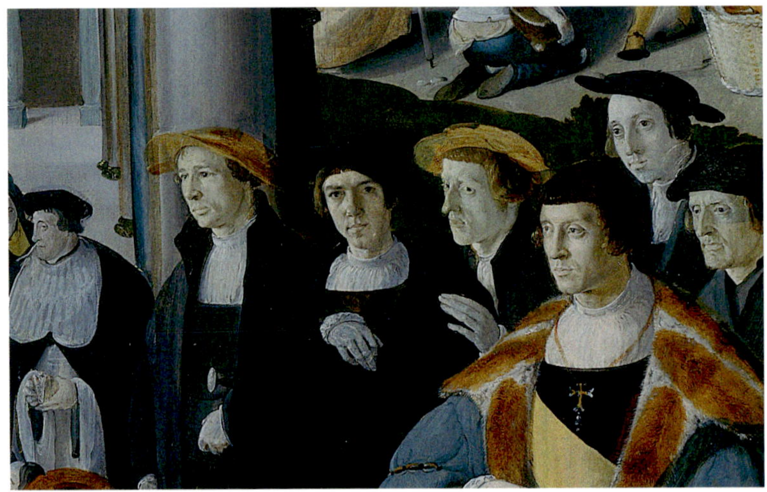

60
Detail of fig. 59 with the group of portraits. The distinctive heads are related to the large portrait drawings that Lucas van Leyden made in 1521.

61
Lucas van Leyden, *Portrait of a man*, 1521. Black chalk, 26 x 35 cm. Stedelijk Museum De Lakenhal, Leiden. This and four other large portrait drawings date from 1521, the year in which Lucas van Leyden and Albrecht Dürer met in Antwerp.

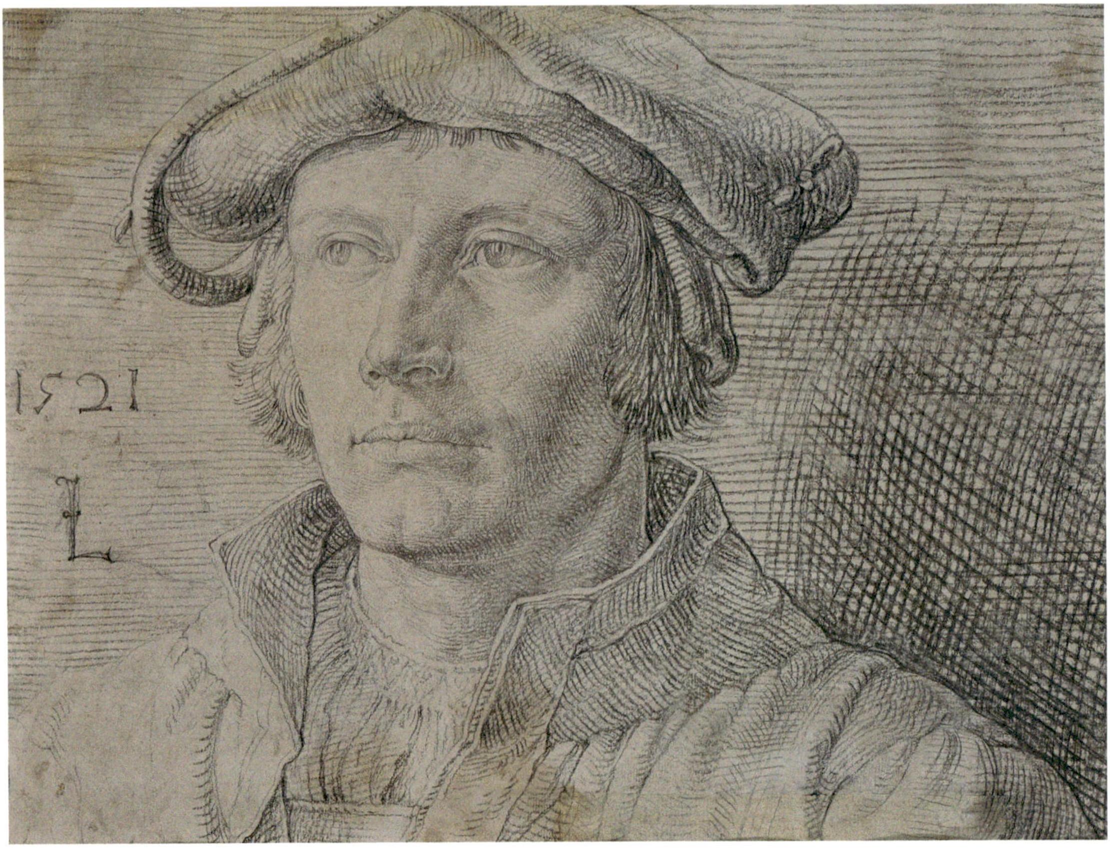

62
Workshop of Lucas van Leyden, *The Virgin and Child*, c. 1530. Oil on panel, 35 x 27.5 cm. Rijksmuseum, Amsterdam. The Rijksmuseum bought this small painting as a Lucas van Leyden from the Schloss Collection in Paris in 1949. The mediocre quality and different painting technique indicate that it is probably a copy made in the artist's workshop. Dendrochronological examination has shown that the panel on which it is painted came from the same tree as the wings of *The dance around the golden calf*. It is a copy after a work related to *The Virgin and Child* in Oslo (fig. 63).

63
Lucas van Leyden, *The Virgin and Child*, c. 1527. Oil on panel, 24.5 x 21.5 cm. Nasjonalmuseet, Oslo. This little picture, which must have been painted in the same period as the *Last Judgement* and *The dance*, has the quality and refinement typical of Lucas van Leyden's work.

Josua Bruyn published an article identifying the scene as *The calling of St Antony* and argued for an attribution to Aertgen Claesz van Leyden (1498-1564), a contemporary of Lucas's. Apart from the L, which turned out to be a later addition, the remarkable group of donors' portraits on the right (fig. 60) was a strong argument for giving the panel to Lucas van Leyden. The exceptional quality of these likenesses immediately recalls the male portraits in black chalk that Lucas made in 1521 (fig. 61). Although the Rijksmuseum abandoned the attribution to Lucas van Leyden long ago, the painting is still very popular with the public. That is not the case with the small *Virgin and Child* (fig. 62), which the museum bought in 1949. It was probably made in Lucas's workshop, but it lacks the quality and refinement of a painting like another small *Virgin and Child* in Oslo (fig. 63).

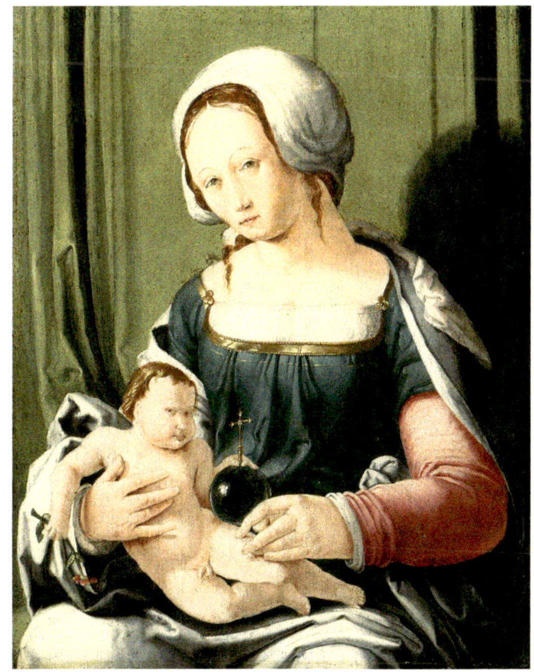

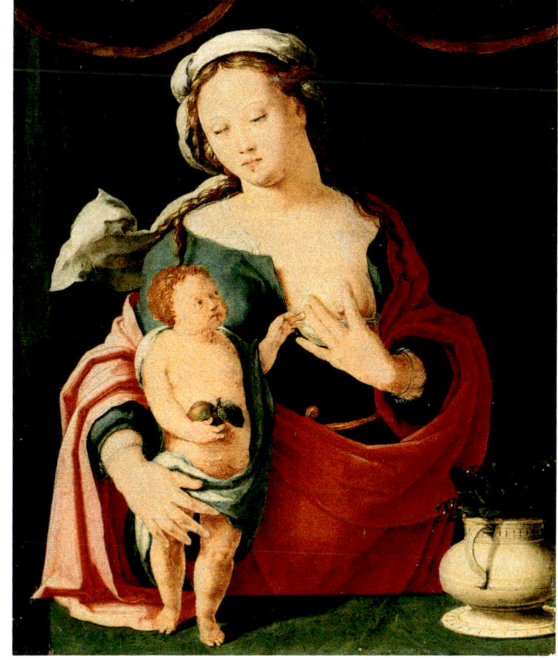

64
Lucas van Leyden, *The Resurrection*, c. 1529. Black chalk, brush in grey and black, 25.2 x 20.1 cm. Rijksmuseum, Amsterdam. This formerly unknown, late drawing by Lucas van Leyden was acquired by the Rijksmuseum in 1982 with support from the Vereniging Rembrandt. Executed with chalk and brush, it is a painstakingly executed design for a painted glass roundel, and the style is very close to other late prints inspired by Italian models.

A FIRST-RATE PURCHASE AND A MISSED OPPORTUNITY

Fortunately, fairly soon after the purchase of the Virgin and Child the museum's wish to own a first-rate painting by Lucas van Leyden was fulfilled with the acquisition of *The dance around the golden calf*. That, though, may have resulted in the failure to acquire another of the artist's key works. At around the same time, *Moses striking water from the rock* of 1527 (fig. 27), which once hung in the Galleria Borghese in Rome and was later in Nuremberg, was on loan to the Rijksmuseum. It was for sale, but the purchase fell through because of the high asking price and the drab look of this canvas painting, which paled in comparison to the radiant appearance of *The dance*. It was acquired in 1954 by the Museum of Fine Arts in Boston. In hindsight it is regrettable that this exceptional, monumental painting was not preserved for the Rijksmuseum.

DRAWINGS BY LUCAS VAN LEYDEN

There are around 30 drawings which can be attributed to Lucas van Leyden with some degree of certainty. Most of them are in Berlin, Paris, and above all London. The Rijksmuseum has only a chalk drawing of a young man from Wtenbogaert's album of prints (fig. 58). In 1982 the museum succeeded in acquiring a superb and hitherto unknown drawing by Lucas, *The Resurrection* (fig. 64). It is a meticulously executed design for a painted glass roundel, and is very close in style to the print series, *The story of Adam and Eve* discussed above (fig. 30 a-b).

The chance of acquiring another first-rate work by Lucas van Leyden is unlikely to come again soon, but in the meantime the Rijksmuseum has a fine ensemble of his works, with *The dance around the golden calf* as its dazzling centrepiece.

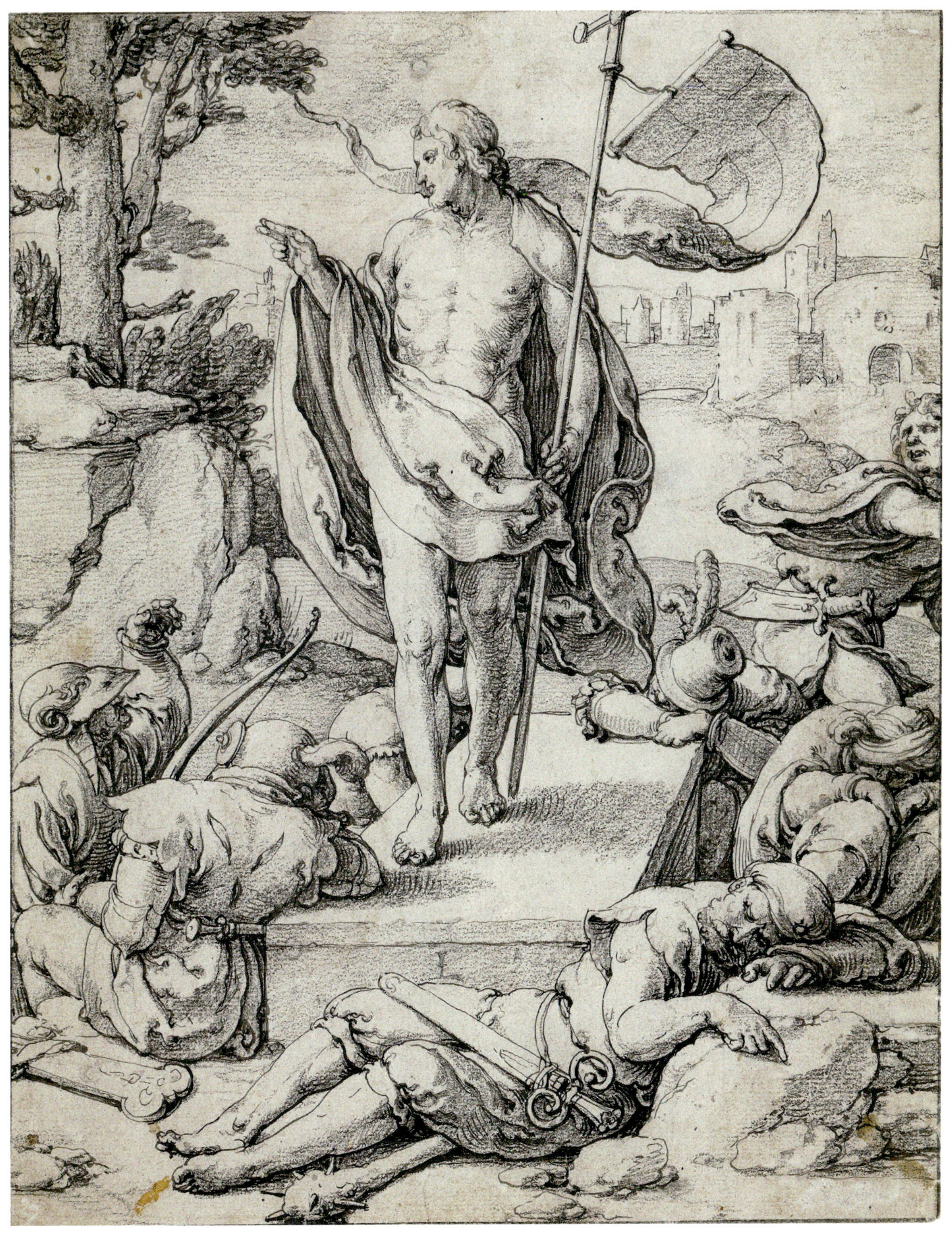

Further reading

The rediscovery of a masterpiece
See N. Beets, 'De dans om het gouden kalf. Een hervonden triptiek van Lucas van Leyden', *Oud Holland* 67 (1952), pp. 183-199, and A. van Schendel, 'Lucas van Leyden's "Dans om het gouden kalf" terug in Amsterdam', *Bulletin van het Rijksmuseum* 1 (1953), pp. 2-8.

The Old Testament story
I am extremely grateful to Prof. Ilja M. Veldman. For the iconography of *The dance around the golden calf* see E. Kirschbaum (ed.), *Lexikon der Christlichen Ikonographie*, 8 vols., Freiburg im Breisgau 1968-1976, vol. 2, cols. 478-482. See also I.M. Veldman, *Images for the eye and soul: function and meaning in Netherlandish prints* (1450-1650), Leiden 2006, pp. 119-150, esp. pp. 119-219.

The life and work of Lucas van Leyden
I used the Dutch transcription of the pages on Lucas van Leyden in Karel van Mander's *Schilder-boeck*, Haarlem 1604, fols. 211r-215r), in R. Vos, *Lucas van Leyden*, Bentveld/Maarssen 1978, pp. 143-146. For an annotated edition of the text see R. Vos, 'The life of Lucas van Leyden by Karel van Mander', *Nederlands Kunsthistorisch Jaarboek* 29 (1978, Lucas van Leyden-studies), pp. 459-507. The English translation, with minor amendations, is from H. Miedema, *Karel van Mander. The lives of the illustrious Netherlandish and German painters*, Doornspijk 1994-1999, vol. 1, pp. 103-119; vol. 3 (1996), pp. 1-31. The full text of *Het Schilder-boeck*, with reproductions of the original pages, can be found at www.dbnl.nl. For Lucas van Leyden's prints see J.P. Filedt Kok, *Lucas van Leyden grafiek*. Amsterdam (Rijksmuseum) 1978, the exhibition catalogue E.S. Jacobowitz and S.L. Stepanek, *The prints of Lucas van Leyden & his contemporaries*, Washington (National Gallery of Art) and Boston (Museum of Fine Arts) 1983, and J.P. Filedt Kok, *The New Hollstein – Dutch & Flemish etchings, engravings and woodcuts 1450-1700 – LUCAS VAN LEYDEN*, Rotterdam/Amsterdam 1996.
For the paintings see J.P. Filedt Kok, 'Underdrawings and other technical aspects in the paintings of Lucas van Leyden', *Nederlands Kunsthistorisch Jaarboek* 29 (1978, Lucas van Leyden-studies), pp. 1-184, and E.L. Smith, *The paintings of Lucas van Leyden – A new appraisal, with catalogue raisonné*, Columbia (Missouri)/London 1992.

The late paintings
For the Munich diptych see J.P. Filedt Kok, P. Eikemeier and J.R.J. van Asperen de Boer, 'Das Diptychon des Lucas van Leyden von 1522 – Versuch einer Rekonstruktion', *Nederlands Kunsthistorisch Jaarboek* 26 (1975), pp. 229-258.
On the triptych in St Petersburg see N. Nikulin, 'Some data concerning the history of the triptych *The healing of the blind man of Jericho* by Lucas van Leyden', *Nederlands Kunsthistorisch Jaarboek* 29 (1978, Lucas van Leyden-studies), pp. 299-310.
On the iconography of the canvas in Boston see Lawrence A. Silver, 'The Sin of Moses: comments on the early Reformation in a late painting by Lucas van Leyden', *The Art Bulletin* 60 (1973), pp. 401-09.

The genesis of *The dance*
For the methods used in the examination of early Netherlandish paintings see J. Dijkstra, 'Technical examination', in B. Ridderbos *et al.* (eds.), *Early Netherlandish paintings. rediscovery, reception and research*, Amsterdam 2001, and M. Faries, 'Reshaping the field: the contribution of technical studies', in M.W. Ainsworth (ed.), *Early Netherlandish painting at the cross-roads: a critical look at current methodologies*

(The Metropolitan Museum of Art Symposia), New York 2001, pp. 70-105. For the technical examination of the paintings of Lucas van Leyden see Filedt Kok 1978, esp. pp. 101-114 on *The dance around the golden calf*, and more generally, J.R.J. van Asperen de Boer, M. Faries and J.P. Filedt Kok, 'Schildertechniek en atelierpraktijk in de zestiende-eeuwse Noord-Nederlandse kunst', in the exhibition catalogue *Kunst voor de beeldenstorm*, Amsterdam (Rijksmuseum) 1986, pp. 85-116. With thanks to Margreet Wolters for her remarks on the colour notations in *The dance.*

The former owners of *The dance*

I am greatly indebted to S.A.C. Dudok van Heel for the information on the seventeenth-century provenance of *The dance*. See also E.W. Moes, 'Aanteekeningen van Mr. Hendrik Houmes op Van Manders Schilder-Boeck', *Oud Holland* 7 (1889), pp. 149-154. On the residents of 214 and 364-370 Herengracht see I.H. van Eeghen *et al.*, *Vier eeuwen Herengracht*, Amsterdam 1976, pp. 470 and 520. A great debt is owed to Huub Baya and Paul van Duin for restoring the 'beautiful cabinet', and to Reinier J. Baarsen for his description of it.

The Rijksmuseum in search of the real Lucas van Leyden

On the collection history of the Rijksmuseum see J.P. Filedt Kok (with the assistance of E. Bergvelt), 'De vroege Nederlandse schilderkunst in het Rijksmuseum', *Bulletin van het Rijksmuseum* 46 (1998), pp. 125-205, and J.P. Filedt Kok, 'Early Netherlandish art in the collections of the Rijksmuseum', in H. van Os *et al.*, *Netherlandish art in the Rijksmuseum 1400-1600*, Zwolle/Amsterdam 2000, pp. 25-40.
On the Wtenbogaert album see J.W. Niemeijer, 'De herkomsten en lotgevallen van de Lucas van Leyden-collectie in het Rijksprentenkabinet', in J.P. Filedt Kok, *Lucas van Leyden grafiek*, Amsterdam (Rijksmuseum) 1978, pp. 7-14.
On Lucas van Leyden's reputation and the collecting of his prints see B. Cornelis and J.P. Filedt Kok, 'Taste for Lucas van Leyden prints', *Simiolus* 26 (1998), pp. 18-86.
For the identification of *The church sermon* and its attribution to Aertgen van Leyden see J. Bruyn, 'Twee St. Antonius-panelen en andere werken van Aertgen van Leyden', *Nederlands Kunsthistorisch Jaarboek* 11 (1960), pp. 36-119.
On the drawings see W.Th. Kloek, 'The drawings of Lucas van Leyden', *Nederlands Kunsthistorisch Jaarboek* 29 (1978, Lucas van Leyden-studies), pp. 425-458, and W.Th. Kloek and J.P. Filedt Kok, 'De opstanding van Christus, getekend door Lucas van Leyden', *Bulletin van het Rijksmuseum* 31 (1983), pp. 4-20.

I am very grateful to Jenny Reynaerts, Marijn Schapelhouman and Ilja M. Veldman for their critical reading of earlier drafts of this book.

Thanks are due to Prof. J.R.J. van Asperen de Boer and the Rijksbureau voor Kunsthistorische Documentatie (RKD, Netherlands Institute for Art History) in The Hague for the infrared reflectogram assemblies reproduced in this book. Edwin Buijsen made the assemblies of details from *The Last Judgement* using reflectograms from the 1970s. Margreet Wolters is responsible for the excellent assemblies of details from *Potiphar's wife* and *The dance around the golden calf*, which she recorded recently.

The dance around the golden calf by Lucas van Leyden is a publication of the Rijksmuseum and Nieuw Amsterdam *Publishers*.

Author
Jan Piet Filedt Kok was Senior Curator of early Netherlandish painting in the Rijksmuseum until April 2008, and is Professor of Workshop Practices at the University of Amsterdam.

Translator
Michael Hoyle

Photography
The Image Department of the Rijksmuseum and other institutions mentioned in the captions. Information to be added to the following illustrations:
fig. 7 RACM, Zeist; fig. 9 RMN/© Jacques Quecq d'Henripret; figs. 16, 19 Bpk, Berlin/ photo Jörg Anders, Gemäldegalerie, Staatliche Museen zu Berlin; fig. 22 Blauel/ Gnamm – ARTOTHEK; figs. 23, 28, 29 ARTOTHEK; fig. 34 IRR: © NWO/Stichting RKD; figs. 35, 36, 37 IRR: © Prof. dr. J.R.J. van Asperen de Boer/Stichting RKD; figs. 38-47 IRR: © Stichting RKD; fig. 50 Hanz Hinz – ARTOTHEK; fig. 51 The Barber Institute of Fine Arts, University of Birmingham/ The Bridgeman Art Library; fig. 53 RMN/ © Gérard Blot; fig. 57 Royal Picture Gallery Mauritshuis, The Hague; fig. 63 photo: J. Lathion © Nasjonalmuseet 2008.

Front cover: Lower half of the centre panel.
Inside front cover: The triptych in its seventeenth-century ebony frame.
Inside back cover: Infrared reflectogram assembly of the underdrawing in the lower half of the centre panel (see front cover).
© Stichting RKD/RM.

Design
Studio Berry Slok, Amsterdam

Lithography
Nauta en Haagen Oss b.v.

Printing
Drukkerij Wilco b.v., Amersfoort

ISBN 978 90 8689 0408
NUR 646

For more information on the activities of the Rijksmuseum and Nieuw Amsterdam, please visit www.rijksmuseum.nl and www.nieuwamsterdam.nl.